Jonathan Edwards
and
the Immediacy of God

Jonathan Edwards and the Immediacy of God

JOHN CARRICK

WIPF & STOCK · Eugene, Oregon

JONATHAN EDWARDS AND THE IMMEDIACY OF GOD

Wipf & Stock
An Imprint of Wipf and Stock Publishers
199 W. 8th Ave., Suite 3
Eugene, OR 97401

www.wipfandstock.com

PAPERBACK ISBN: 978-1-7252-5291-2
HARDCOVER ISBN: 978-1-7252-5292-9
EBOOK ISBN: 978-1-7252-5293-6

12/07/20

To

Paul Helm:

mentor and friend

Contents

Acknowledgments

I wish to express my thanks to the Mack Library of Bob Jones University in Greenville, SC. I am very grateful to have been able to taste of the riches of this fine library during the course of the writing of this book.

I would also like to thank my student-friend, Josh Malinowski, from North Greenville University, for his kind help with various computer issues. His ready assistance in this project is greatly appreciated.

I would like to thank my friend, Dr. Bill Ryan, who has kindly helped me with various suggestions relating to the content and also the formatting of this book. I am grateful to him for his friendly assistance.

I also wish to express my gratitude to Paul Helm in two significant respects: it was he who first suggested to me that the theme of the immediacy of God in the thought of Jonathan Edwards might prove to be a fruitful and rewarding study—I have, in fact, found this theme to be an enthralling study; and it has been he who, throughout the years of writing, has been unfailingly kind and helpful as a mentor. It is to him that I dedicate this book.

INTRODUCTION

THE YEARS 1675 TO 1711, observes Norman Fiering in *Jonathan Edwards's Moral Thought and Its British Context* (1981), constitute, from the intellectual standpoint, a period of "great fertility and interchange in ideas."[1] It was during this period of thirty-six years that some of the great seminal works of modern intellectual history were published: Nicolas Malebranche's *De la recherche de la vérité* (1675); Isaac Newton's *Principia* (1687); John Locke's *Essay Concerning Human Understanding* (1689); Archbishop Tillotson's latitudinarian sermons, including *Of the Eternity of Hell-Torments* (1690); two separate, independent English translations of Malebranche's work, entitled *The Search after Truth* (1694); John Toland's *Christianity Not Mysterious* (1696); Samuel Clarke's famous Boyle lectures, published as *Demonstration of the Being and Attributes of God* (1705); Gottfried Wilhelm Leibniz's *Théodicée* (1710); George Berkeley's *Treatise Concerning the Principles of Human Knowledge* (1710); Pierre Bayle's *Dictionary*, in English translation (1710); and the third Earl of Shaftesbury's *Characteristics* (1711). Indeed, Fiering describes this era as "the great watershed period in British and Continental thought."[2]

It was, moreover, during this period that some of the most significant movements in religious history developed. The last quarter of the seventeenth century witnessed the consolidation of Quakerism in the American Colonies, the emergence of Stoddardism[3] within the Congregational

1. Fiering, *Jonathan Edwards's Moral Thought*, 15.

2. Fiering, *Jonathan Edwards's Moral Thought*, 14.

3. "Stoddardism" is the term given to the ecclesiastical innovation of "open communion" which was introduced into the Northampton church in 1677 by Edwards's maternal grandfather and ministerial predecessor, Solomon Stoddard.

churches of New England, and the rise of deism in Old England. Fascinatingly, these works and these movements set the stage for some of the most significant tensions, controversies, and debates of the early and mid-eighteenth century Enlightenment. Powerful winds of change were blowing across the Atlantic from Europe and also from within New England: it was the age of Malebranche, the age of Newton, the age of Locke, the age of Tillotson, the age of the Scientific Revolution, the age of deism, the age of Stoddardism, the age of Quakerism, the age of rising antipathy towards "enthusiasm," and the age of Berkeley's immaterialism. We should not fail to note that it was during this period and into such a world—a world of very significant intellectual and religious ferment—that Jonathan Edwards was born on October 5, 1703.

"In 1700," contends Bertrand Russell, "the mental outlook of educated men was completely modern; in 1600, except among a very few, it was still largely medieval."[4] The crucial factor in this remarkable transition was the Newtonian revolution, the pivotal event of which was the publication of Isaac Newton's *Principia* (1687). At the outset of the seventeenth century, the Ptolemaic (geocentric) system, although shaken by the Copernican (heliocentric) system, still reigned supreme; by the commencement of the eighteenth century, the Ptolemaic monolith had been toppled. Edwards himself, in his youthful writings, refers to the now-superseded Ptolemaic system: "Thus some men will yet say that they cannot conceive how the fixed stars can be so distant as that the earth's annual revolution should cause no parallax among them, and so are almost ready to fall back into antiquated Ptolemy, his system, merely to ease their imagination."[5] The astonishing absence of stellar parallax in a heliocentric system merely demonstrated the inconceivable vastness of the universe.

Newton's confirmation of the Copernican system was, however, construed by certain minds as a confirmation of a deistic distancing of God. Douglas J. Elwood notes the impact of the Newtonian revolution upon theology and faith: "While this marked an advance in experimental science, it had disastrous consequences outside the domain of pure science. God was pushed to the periphery of the knowable universe and relegated to the beginning of the temporal process . . . Thus the deistic view of God arose."[6] Edwards's response to this deistic distancing of God was *inter alia* (amongst other things) that of highlighting, in a quite extraordinary manner, the concept of the immediacy of God. Indeed, Edwards's consistent, pervasive, and

4. Russell, *Western Philosophy*, 536.
5. Edwards, *Scientific and Philosophical Writings*, 197.
6. Elwood, *Philosophical Theology*, 49–50.

multifaceted emphasis upon the concept of divine immediacy throughout the various aspects of his *oeuvre* constitutes, on his part, a lifelong counterblast to deism.

This concept of the immediacy of God is perhaps best understood in terms of the classic scholastic distinction between primary and secondary causation—a distinction that is adopted unreservedly by the Westminster Confession of Faith (1646):

Chapter 3: *Of God's Eternal Decree*

1. God, from all eternity, did, by the most wise and holy counsel of his own will, freely, and unchangeably ordain whatsoever comes to pass: yet so, as thereby neither is God the author of sin, nor is violence offered to the will of the creatures, nor is the liberty or contingency of second causes taken away, but rather established.

Chapter 5: *Of Providence*

1. God the great Creator of all things doth uphold, direct, dispose, and govern all creatures, actions, and things, from the greatest even to the least, by his most wise and holy providence.
2. Although, in relation to the foreknowledge and decree of God, the First Cause, all things come to pass immutably, and infallibly; yet, by the same providence, he ordereth them to fall out, according to the nature of second causes, either necessarily, freely, or contingently.
3. God, in his ordinary providence, maketh use of means, yet is free to work without, above, and against them, at his pleasure.

It should be noted that the Westminster Confession of Faith makes a decisive distinction here between "the First Cause" on the one hand and "second causes" or "means" on the other. According to this distinction, God is the First Cause or the immediate cause of *x* when God brings about *x* without the employment, intervention, or cooperation of any intermediate causes. Thus God is, clearly, the First Cause or the immediate Cause in the creation of the sun in the beginning; but it is generally accepted that, in the ongoing gravitational pull exerted by the sun throughout the solar system, God makes use of intermediate or "second causes"; namely, the force of gravity, or what Edwards himself refers to variously as "solidity," "matter acting upon matter," or "natural necessity."[7] It is important to note that there is a strong emphasis in the Confession upon the reality and the integrity of

7. Edwards, *Freedom of the Will*, 157.

"second causes": "God, the First Cause, . . . by the same providence, . . . ordereth them to fall out, according to the nature of second causes"; and "God, in his ordinary providence, maketh use of means." It should be noted that, while creation is clearly attributed here to the First Cause, and while there is an emphasis upon the ever-potential immediacy of God (as in miracles, for instance)—"God . . . is free to work without, above, and against them, at his pleasure"—God's works of providence are, in general, attributed to second causes. Interestingly, the main emphasis of the Confession falls not so much upon the First Cause as upon second causes; in other terms, it falls not so much upon immediacy as upon mediacy or means. The Confession's clear distinction between the First Cause and second causes, a distinction also implicitly made by the Scriptures, certainly has no brief for an occasionalism in which second causes are effectively swallowed up by the First Cause.

The theme of the immediacy of God in Edwards's thought has been explored by Douglas J. Elwood in *The Philosophical Theology of Jonathan Edwards*. This theme of divine immediacy, Elwood contends, constitutes the "controlling idea"[8] and "the principle of correlation"[9] in Edwards's philosophical-theological system. "His whole theology stands out against all forms of deism, abstract theism, or nonmystical orthodoxy, then and now; it rises in opposition to any view that tends to separate God from the world he has made."[10] Indeed, Elwood is convinced that Edwards's profound preoccupation with this theme lures him powerfully in the direction of panentheism: "In Edwards we find a delicate balance of traditional theistic and classical pantheistic elements, which can only be called a variety of panentheism."[11] Elwood contends that Edwards, in seeking to steer a careful *via media* between traditional theism and classical pantheism, was searching for "a theology of the 'third way.'"[12]

Elwood's central thesis concerning divine immediacy can and should be developed further, both intensively and extensively. Thus the whole issue of Edwards's concept of time and eternity, and the relationship between this concept and the issue of divine immediacy, should be explored. In the first chapter, we will note the relationship between the putative atemporality of God and the concept of the immediacy of God. We will explore Edwards's precocious preoccupation, as a student at Yale, with what he terms "the

8. Elwood, *Philosophical Theology*, 90.
9. Elwood, *Philosophical Theology*, 3.
10. Elwood, *Philosophical Theology*, 9.
11. Elwood, *Philosophical Theology*, 57.
12. Elwood, *Philosophical Theology*, 7.

immediate exercise of divine power" throughout the created realm.[13] This notion inevitably raises the question as to whether the concept of "mechanism" in the government of the cosmos is a reality, or whether this concept, and the related concept of "second causes," is, effectively, an illusion. We thus face, inevitably, the possibility of occasionalism in Edwards's philosophical-theological system—a possibility that intensifies in the light of his doctrine of continuous creation. Indeed, it appears that Edwards's concept of continuous creation yields, inevitably, a doctrine of temporal parts. At this point, we will note the influence of Nicolas Malebranche's remarkable theocentrism upon Edwards's system. We will then explore what might be termed "the problem of infinity," Edwards's apparent attraction to the concept of "inclusive infinity," and also the question as to whether or not the strong Neoplatonic elements in his system yield a panentheism in which all things are "contained in God."

In the second chapter, we will note the remarkable, indeed mysterious, absence of emphasis upon divine immediacy in Edwards's great treatise, *Freedom of the Will*. We also explore the *prima facie* (at first glance) tension between the horizontal determinism that dominates this treatise and the vertical occasionalism with which his thought as a whole is suffused. Although, as the treatise unfolds, Edwards's horizontal determinism fuses almost seamlessly, along compatibilist lines, with his vertical determinism, the apparent incompatibility between his horizontal determinism and his vertical occasionalism persists. Thus we will note the way in which Edwards's *creatio continua-cum*-occasionalism doctrine appears to entail significant problems for Edwards's metaphysics of sin, and most notably with regard to the question as to whether Edwards's God is, on Edwards's own premises, the author of sin. We will explore the possibility that the anomaly of Edwards's determinism-*cum*-occasionalism position might possibly be resolved via the theory that Edwards is, in fact, writing at two different levels, each of which is legitimate in its own sphere. Such a two-tiered approach would explain Edwards's ambivalence with regard to both mechanism and means. In this context, we will explore the fascinatingly cautious terms in which Edwards expresses his concept of causation in *Freedom of the Will*. We will also note that, if, as is the case, Edwards's normal emphasis upon divine immediacy is significantly suppressed in this treatise, the anti-deistic strain is nevertheless powerfully present. One of Edwards's great targets in this emphasis upon the immediacy of God is, unquestionably, what he clearly regarded as the pernicious gradualism of the Arminian scheme; one of Edwards's great objectives in this emphasis upon the immediacy of God

13. Edwards, *Scientific and Philosophical Writings*, 215–16.

is that of safeguarding the divine, sovereign, and supernatural nature of the act of regeneration by the Spirit of God.

In the third chapter, we will explore a significant strand within the over-arching theme of divine immediacy which is not addressed by Elwood; namely, Edwards's position in the communion controversy of 1749–50. To that end, it is necessary to trace the relatively rapid unraveling of "the New England experiment" of the 1630s and 40s and the emergence of the compromise systems of the Halfway Covenant in 1662 and of Stoddardism in 1677. This experiment in the churches of New England had been rooted in the ideal of ecclesiastical purity—a purity that expressed itself in exclusiveness. But both the Halfway Covenant and Stoddardism were clearly characterized by a conception of the church of Christ that was far more relaxed, inclusive, and comprehensive than that of the earlier New England ideal. Negatively, Edwards's great concern in the communion controversy was that these compromise systems had simply fostered the externalization of religion and the externalization of God and had thus distanced God from the church; positively, Edwards's great concern was that participants in the Lord's Supper should be characterized by "the consent of our hearts" and "the consent of our wills."[14] Edwards's entire position in this controversy reflects the Puritan preoccupation with "immediacy in relation to God," and thus reflects his obvious concern to safeguard a certain type of piety; namely, the piety of the experimental Calvinistic tradition.

In the fourth chapter, "Spiritual Experience," we will explore the phenomenon of "enthusiasm" and its relationship to the concept of immediacy. We will note that the issue of "enthusiasm" lies at the very center of Quakerism, with its notion of "the light within," and also that certain Quaker-like traits and tendencies were manifested by many involved in the Great Awakening of the 1740s. Moreover, Edwards's inveterate opposition to Quakerism demonstrates the very important fact that his commitment to the concept of immediacy was not boundless. We note, therefore, that Edwards was throughout his life fighting a battle on two fronts; namely, against the anti-immediacy position of the deists on the one hand, and the ultra-immediacy position of the enthusiasts on the other. If the Quakers represent the latter position, Charles Chauncy represents the former position—one that Edwards pointedly describes as that of "standing aloof" or "standing at a distance" from the phenomenon of revival. Pivotal to Edwards's views on spiritual experience in general, and to his doctrine of regeneration in particular, is his concept of "the sense of the heart." Thus we note again Edwards's persistent emphasis upon the heart and the crucial connection

14. Edwards, *Ecclesiastical Writings*, 205.

between the heart and the concept of immediacy. Indeed, there is a striking parallel between the concept of "the sense of the heart" in the realm of spiritual experience and the concept of "the consent of the heart" in the realm of the Lord's Supper and ecclesiology.

There is, unquestionably, a powerful individualism about Edwards's entire position on spiritual experience, and this individualism coheres with the theme of the immediacy of God and with the related theme of immediacy in relation to God. It should be noted, however, that Edwards's emphasis upon the theme of the immediacy of God lies within the orbit of the Word-and-Spirit approach of conservative Puritanism. There is, throughout his *oeuvre,* a very powerful, yet measured, emphasis upon the Spirit of God, and it is fascinating to note that his emphasis upon divine immediacy in this sphere is, in fact, marked by somewhat less exuberance and somewhat greater restraint than his emphasis upon divine immediacy in the sphere of God and the creation. It is important to note that, in the sphere of spiritual experience, Edwards does not allow his penchant for the concept of divine immediacy to run riot—he does not fall foul of what John Locke aptly describes as "the ungrounded fancies of a man's own brain."[15]

15. Locke, *Human Understanding*, 451.

GOD AND THE CREATION

ETERNITY AND TIME

It is perhaps appropriate to commence an analysis of Jonathan Edwards's view of God's relationship to the creation by considering his concept of eternity, and thus his concept of God's relation to time. In this context, Paul Helm notes that "there have been two broad traditions of thought about God's relation to time; some have argued that God exists at all times and, since he exists necessarily, he is backwardly and forwardly everlasting."[1] This was the position held, it appears, by William of Ockham (c. 1287–1347) in the medieval period and is the position held by Richard Swinburne and many other modern scholars.[2] Thus God is viewed here as without beginning, without end, but *not* without succession. According to this view, God is characterized by succession—he has a past, a present, and a future. Herman Bavinck explains that this view was the position of the deists:

> Deism . . . defines eternity as time extended infinitely in both directions; according to it, the difference between eternity and time is quantitative, not qualitative; gradual, not essential; the distinction is not that eternity excludes a succession of moments, but merely that it excludes a beginning and an end; past, present, and future are terms that should be applied to God as well as to man. The Socinians held this view, and so did many after them.[3]

1. Helm, *Faith and Understanding*, 87.
2. Helm, *Faith and Understanding*, 87.
3. Bavinck, *Doctrine of God*, 154.

This concept of eternity as "everlastingness" necessarily implies that, at a certain point along the infinitely extended line of time, God created the cosmos. Thus the cosmos was, according to this position, created *in tempore* (in time).

"Others, such as Boethius, and of course Augustine," notes Helm, "argue that God exists in a timeless eternity. He cannot have a past or future, for such change is incompatible with the divine fullness of being. So according to Augustine God creates the universe not in time, but with time."[4] God is viewed here as without beginning, without end, *and* without succession. This concept of eternity as "timelessness" or "successionlessness" is captured by Boethius's celebrated definition: *Vitae interminabilis, tota, simul, et perfecta possessio—the total, simultaneous, and perfect comprehension of endless existence.* This concept of the atemporality of God necessarily entails the position that, prior to the creation of the cosmos (if we may so speak), time did not exist. Thus the cosmos was, according to this position, created *cum tempore* (with time).

In his commentary, *The Literal Meaning of Genesis,* Augustine (354–430 AD) makes this statement concerning time and creation:

> With the motion of creatures, time began to run its course. It is idle to look for time before creation, as if time can be found before time. If there were no motion of either a spiritual or corporeal creature, by which the future moving through the present would succeed the past, there would be no time at all. A creature could not move if it did not exist. We should, therefore, say that time began with creation rather than that creation began with time. But both are from God. For from Him and through Him and in Him are all things.[5]

Augustine's position here is that time did not exist *before* creation. "Time began with creation,"[6] he insists. "We should, therefore, say that time began with creation rather than that creation began with time."[7] Thus there is a sense in which we might describe Augustine's position more precisely as

4. Helm, *Faith and Understanding,* 88. See also Hepburn, "Creation, Religious Doctrine of," in Encyclopedia of Philosophy. "The Christian doctrine bypasses certain formidable difficulties by affirming that the world was created along with, not in, time. It does not force upon us the notion of a time without events. God's eternity is not to be taken as endless temporal duration but as something qualitatively different—a completeness and changelessness that knows none of the successiveness of temporal experience with its 'yet' and 'no longer.'"

5. Augustine, *Genesis,* 153–54.

6. Augustine, *Genesis,* 154.

7. Augustine, *Genesis,* 154.

that of *cum creatione* rather than *cum tempore.* "He made that which gave time its beginning."[8] Thus time is inseparably associated with creation, motion, change, and succession. "Time," observes Bavinck, "is the concomitant of created existence."[9]

It is in his *Confessions* that Augustine addresses the counterpart of this position; namely, the eternity of God. Creation began *cum tempore,* or rather time began *cum creatione.* "O Lord," Augustine writes, "you are outside time in eternity."[10] "You are the Maker of all time."[11] "It is in eternity, which is supreme over time because it is a never-ending present, that you are at once before all past time and after all future time."[12] "In eternity nothing moves into the past: all is present."[13] This means that God does not exist segment by segment. God is outside of time; he transcends time; he is a timelessly eternal being. God inhabits eternity, and this eternity is likened to "a never-ending present." "All is present," insists Augustine. Thus the classic Augustinian-Boethian position insists upon the timeless eternality or successionlessness of God.

GOD'S KNOWLEDGE

It is important to note that in *Freedom of the Will* (1754) Edwards cites Boethius's famous dictum, with approval, twice. At the point of his first citation, Edwards is concerned to emphasize that "there is no succession in God's knowledge,"[14] and that "there is no succession in his ideas or judgment."[15] He writes:

> The very reason why God's knowledge is without succession, is, because it is absolutely perfect, to the highest possible degree of clearness and certainty: all things, whether past, present or to come, being viewed with equal evidence and fullness; future things being seen with as much clearness, as if they were present; the view is always in absolute perfection; and absolute constant perfection admits of no alteration, and so no succession.[16]

8. Augustine, *Genesis*, 154.
9. Bavinck, *Doctrine of God*, 157.
10. Augustine, *Confessions*, 253.
11. Augustine, *Confessions*, 263.
12. Augustine, *Confessions*, 263.
13. Augustine, *Confessions*, 261.
14. Edwards, *Freedom of the Will*, 266.
15. Edwards, *Freedom of the Will*, 267.
16. Edwards, *Freedom of the Will*, 267–68.

> Nothing is more impossible than that the immutable God should be changed, by the succession of time; who comprehends all things, from eternity to eternity, in one, most perfect, and unalterable view; so that his whole eternal duration is *vitae interminabilis, tota, simul* and *perfecta possessio.*[17]

It should be noted, moreover, that not only does Edwards specifically endorse here the Boethian formula with regard to God's timeless eternity; he also specifically rejects the deistic notion of "an infinite length of time before the world was created, distinguished by successive parts,"[18] describing this notion as "a groundless imagination"[19]:

> This objection supposes an infinite length of time before the world was created, distinguished by successive parts, properly and truly so; or a succession of limited and measurable periods of time, following one another, in an infinitely long series: which must needs be a groundless imagination. The eternal duration which was before the world, being only the eternity of God's existence; which is nothing else but his immediate, perfect, and invariable possession of the whole of his unlimited life, together and at once; *vitae interminabilis, tota, simul et perfecta possessio.*[20]

In this passage Edwards unequivocally rejects the *in tempore* position of the deists and unequivocally endorses the *cum tempore* position of Augustine. It will be noted that, in contradistinction to the deists, Edwards views the difference between eternity and time not as quantitative, but as qualitative—the difference is not gradual, but essential. Eternity is perceived not merely as "everlastingness," but also as "timelessness" or "successionlessness."

In *Freedom of the Will,* Edwards goes on to develop some of the implications of this classic position: "Nothing is new to God, in any respect," he insists, "but all things are perfectly and equally in his view from eternity."[21] "No designs of God are new."[22] He adds:

> 'Tis as improper, to imagine that the immensity and omnipresence of God is distinguished by a series of miles and leagues, one beyond another; as that the infinite duration of God is

17. Edwards, *Freedom of the Will*, 268.
18. Edwards, *Freedom of the Will*, 385.
19. Edwards, *Freedom of the Will*, 385.
20. Edwards, *Freedom of the Will*, 385–86.
21. Edwards, *Freedom of the Will*, 434.
22. Edwards, *Freedom of the Will*, 435.

> distinguished by months and years, one after another . . . 'Tis equally improper, to talk of months and years of the divine existence, and mile-squares of deity.[23]

In *God's Chief End in Creation* (provisionally completed in 1756 and published posthumously nine years later), Edwards provides conclusive corroboratory evidence of the consistency of his belief that God is a timelessly eternal being:

> Another thing signified by these expressions of Scripture is that nothing that is from the creature adds to or alters God's happiness, as though it were changeable either by increase or diminution . . . For though these communications of God, these exercises, operations, effects and expressions of his glorious perfections, which God rejoices in, are in time; yet his joy in them is without beginning or change. They were always equally present in the divine mind, He beheld them with equal clearness, certainty, and fullness, in every respect, as he doth now. They were always equally present, as with him there is no variableness or succession. He ever beheld and enjoyed them perfectly in his own independent and immutable power and will.[24]

It is important to note that this passage is in perfect harmony with the citation from Boethius. On the one hand, Edwards insists here that "these communications of God . . . are in time"; on the other hand, he also insists that "his joy in them is without beginning or change. They were always equally present in the divine mind." There can be no question but that Edwards endorses the Augustinian-Boethian position of God's atemporality, together with its inevitable corollary: *Vitae interminabilis, tota, simul, et perfecta possessio.* Edwards clearly aligns himself here with the tradition that extends from Augustine and Boethius to Calvin and the Puritans in general. But the interesting question is this: Has Edwards perhaps detected an implication of the concept of the atemporality of God which had been overlooked by others in this tradition—an implication with regard to the immediacy of God, which, in the age of deism and *contra* deism, needed, in his view, to be highlighted?

What, then, is the corollary of Edwards's endorsement of the *cum tempore* position? It is, surely, that those events which unfold, successively, in the course of history, many of which Edwards himself describes in his *History of the Work of Redemption,* are all immediately present to God: the six days of creation, the fall of humanity, the Flood in the days of Noah, the calling of

23. Edwards, *Freedom of the Will*, 386–87.

24. Edwards, *Ethical Writings*, 448.

Abraham, the Exodus, the entrance into Canaan, the days of the judges, the days of the kings, the days of Elijah and Elisha, the fall of Jerusalem in 586 BC, the seventy years of the Exile, the return under Zerubbabel, Haman's attempted annihilation of the Jews, the rebuilding of the Temple, the birth of John the Baptist, the Incarnation of Christ, the miracles of Christ, the treachery of Judas, the crucifixion, burial, and resurrection of Christ, his ascension into heaven, the destruction of Jerusalem in 70 AD, the rise of the Church of Rome, the Battle of Hastings in 1066, the Reformation of the sixteenth century, the rise of Quakerism, the publication of Isaac Newton's *Principia* in 1687, the Age of the Enlightenment, the Great Awakening in New England, the communion controversy in Northampton in 1749–50, the French Revolution of 1789, the rise of liberal theology in Germany in the nineteenth century, the Great War of 1914–18, the Second World War of 1939–45, the events of September 11, 2001, the second advent of Christ in glory, and the day of judgment—all these events, whether sacred or secular, whether holy or profane, in all of their vastly multitudinous details, are equally and immediately present to God. God timelessly *is*; God timelessly *knows*.

At first glance, Edwards's obvious espousal of the Augustinian-Boethian position with regard to eternity and time would appear to enhance the concept of the immediacy of God. After all, if God is characterized by *the total, simultaneous, and perfect comprehension of endless existence,* as Edwards emphatically affirms, then he is characterized by immediate and perfect perception or knowledge. This is precisely the point that Boethius himself makes:

> Since the state of God is ever that of eternal presence, His knowledge, too, transcends all temporal change and abides in the immediacy of his presence. It embraces all the infinite recesses of past and future and views them in the immediacy of its knowing as though they are happening in the present. If you wish to consider, then, the foreknowledge or prevision by which He discovers all things, it will be more correct to think of it not as a kind of foreknowledge of the future, but as the knowledge of a never ending presence. So that it is better called providence or "looking forth" than prevision or "seeing beforehand." For it is far removed from matters below and looks forth at all things as though from a lofty peak above them.[25]

Helm notes that this Boethian notion of immediate perception involves, in fact, a double immediacy on God's part. God's perception or knowledge is

25. Watts, *Consolation of Philosophy*, 134.

immediate, not only in the sense that it is non-sequential (it is perception without sequence), but also in the sense that it is non-inferential (it is perception without inference). This latter aspect of God's immediacy is rooted in what Helm describes as "the epistemic powers of the knower,"[26] and since the knower is, in this case, God (as opposed to animals or humans), his perception or knowledge is "without the intervention of any inferential element."[27] Helm explains Boethius's position with regard to this sort of immediacy:

> It is knowledge "free from all corporeal influence." Beings in this position do not have to react to external stimuli in order to perceive things. Integral to Boethius's account is a hierarchical view of knowledge according to which the manner in which non-human animals know (by imagination) is different from the way in which humans know (by reason), and how humans know is different from the way in which God knows (by intelligence). Divine knowledge has "boundless immediacy."[28]

Classically, God's knowledge has been construed as *scientia simplicis intelligentiae* (the knowledge of pure intelligence). God's knowledge is not inferential or deductive; it is not demonstrative or discursive; it is not the result of observation or ratiocination. It is innate and intuitive. God knows all things, not by analysis, but by genesis. God's knowledge is thus immediate, not only in the sense that it is non-sequential, but also in the sense that it is non-inferential. Moreover, the etymology of the word "immediate" demonstrates that the word enjoys a *double entendre* which is of great interest at this very point. At a more superficial level, the word "immediate" denotes that which is *without time;* at a more profound level, the word denotes that which is *without means.* These two meanings of the word are intimately related, both causally and semantically. It is precisely because, in certain situations, no means are involved that no time is involved—the employment of means inevitably requires the passage of time. Thus the very absence of means entails the absence of time. God's knowledge is immediate in both senses of the word: it is immediate in the sense that it is independent of time (non-sequential); it is also im-mediate [*sic*] in the sense that it is independent of means (non-inferential).

But does this endorsement of the Augustinian-Boethian position on Edwards's part necessarily require an unmitigated commitment to the concept of divine immediacy at all levels? Does the concept of the *punctum*

26. Helm, "Eternity and Vision in Boethius," 90.
27. Helm, "Eternity and Vision in Boethius," 90.
28. Helm, "Eternity and Vision in Boethius," 91.

stans (the standing point) of God's timeless eternity enhance the concept of God's immanence or does it enhance that of God's transcendence? On the one hand, it is important to note the consequences of this position with regard to the immediacy of God's perception or knowledge; on the other hand, it is important to note that this particular aspect of divine immediacy is perfectly compatible with an emphasis upon the transcendence of God. This position, in and of itself, emphasizes that God is transcendent above time; but does it emphasize that God is immanent in time? After all, immediate perception does not necessarily entail immediate involvement. In fact, Boethius himself concedes that such immediacy of knowledge or perception is compatible with its being "far removed from matters below"; it is compatible with its operating "as though from a lofty peak above them." Indeed, God's immediate perception of all things might conceivably be compatible with what Helm has described as "a kind of Platonic deism":

> Boethius was bent on safeguarding divine omniscience and human freedom in a situation in which God is not envisaged as interacting with his human creatures but as eternally commanding and decreeing. Boethian theology at this point is a kind of Platonic deism.[29]

It is evident, then, that, while the Augustinian-Boethian position with regard to eternity and time is compatible with a certain aspect of divine immediacy, it does not, in and of itself, necessarily entail that multiformity of divine immediacy which is so evident in Edwards's *oeuvre* as a whole. All may be present to God; nothing may lie outside of God's view; but how involved is he in the life of the world? The Augustinian-Boethian position with regard to eternity and time certainly emphasizes the immediacy of God's perception or knowledge, and this coheres with God's omniscience; but God's omniscience in this construction is theoretically compatible with the notion of God's distance from the world—it is theoretically compatible with a kind of deistic, uninvolved transcendence. Paradoxically, the concept of immediacy is, at this point, theoretically compatible with the concept of distance.

"THE IMMEDIATE EXERCISE OF GOD'S POWER"

But the notion of the metaphysical distance of God from the cosmos, so popular in the age of deism into which he was born, was anathema to Jonathan Edwards. Indeed, Edwards displays in his earliest writings profound

29. Helm, *Eternal God*, xii–xiii.

convictions with regard to the immediacy of God in relation to the physical, natural world. The series of propositions and corollaries, since entitled "Of Atoms," was, according to Wallace E. Anderson, probably written in his first year of graduate study, towards the end of 1720.[30] Edwards was, at this point in his academic career at Yale, just seventeen. The following passage demonstrates his precocious preoccupation with the concept of divine immediacy:

Corol. 8. Since . . . solidity [and] indivisibility are the same, and since . . . indivisibility is from the immediate exercise of God's power, it follows that solidity results from the immediate exercise of God's power, causing there to be indefinite resistance in that place where it is.

Corol. 9. Since . . . body and solidity are the same, and . . . solidity is from the immediate exercise of divine power, it follows that all body is nothing but what immediately results from the exercise of divine power in such a particular manner.[31]

Corol. 11. Since . . . body and solidity are the same, and . . . resistance or solidity are by the immediate exercise of divine power, it follows that the certain unknown substance, which philosophers used to think subsisted by itself, and stood underneath and kept up solidity and all other properties, which they used to say it was impossible for a man to have an idea of, is nothing at all distinct from solidity itself; or, if they must needs apply that word to something else that does really and properly subsist by itself and support all properties, they must apply it to the divine Being or power itself. And here I believe all those philosophers would apply it, if they knew what they meant themselves. So that the substance of bodies at last becomes either nothing, or nothing but the Deity acting in that particular manner in those parts of space where he thinks fit. So that, speaking most strictly, there is no proper substance but God himself . . . How truly, then, is he said to be *ens entium*.

Corol. 12. Since . . . solidity or body is immediately from the exercise of divine power, causing there to be resistance in such a part of space, it follows that motion also, which is the communication of body, solidity, or this resistance, from one part of space to another successively . . . is from the immediate exercise of divine power so communicating that resistance, according to certain conditions which we call the laws of motion. How truly then is it that in him we live, move, and have our being.

30. Edwards, *Scientific and Philosophical Writings*, 186.

31. Edwards, *Scientific and Philosophical Writings*, 214–15.

Corol. 13. From all which, we find that what divines used to say concerning divine concourse had a great deal of truth lay at the bottom of it.[32]

The crucial *leitmotiv* in this passage is that of "the immediate exercise of God's power" or "the immediate exercise of divine power." Edwards insists in these Corollaries that *body, solidity, indivisibility, resistance,* and *motion* in the natural world are not properties which, subsequent to the initial act of creation, now subsist independently of the Creator, but rather are properties which are directly attributable to the immediate power of God. Edwards denies here that there is, as Locke puts it, a "certain unknown substance, which philosophers used to think subsisted by itself, and stood underneath and kept up solidity and all other properties."[33] Interestingly, Edwards engages here in an implicit critique of Locke's definition of "substance" as "something, he knows not what."[34] In his celebrated *Essay Concerning Human Understanding* (1689) Locke had acknowledged his ignorance with regard to that which upholds all things in the creation. Over against the vagueness of Locke's definition of substance, Edwards formally identifies "substance" as "the divine Being or power itself": "So that, speaking most strictly, there is no proper substance but God himself . . . How truly, then, is he said to be *ens entium*." For Edwards "substance" denotes "that which exists by itself." In other words, God is absolutely independent—God alone, insists Edwards, exists *a se* (by himself or from himself). Thus the reference to God as *ens entium* (the being of beings) should be construed not merely in a superlative sense, but also in the sense that God himself is the very being, the very essence, the very substance of all beings—their very existence and all their characteristics are absolutely and immediately dependent upon the Creator himself.

Moreover, in "Things to be Considered and Written fully about," completed *circa* 1723, Edwards deals with the concept of *gravity* in similar vein:

22. Solidity is gravity; so that, in some sense, the essence of bodies is gravity: and to shew how the very bare being of body, without supposing harmonious being, necessarily infers gravity. And to observe that folly of seeking for a mechanical cause of gravity; but to observe that this has as much a mechanical cause as anything in the world, and is as philosophically to be solved, and ought no more to be attributed to the immediate operation of God than everything else, which indeed arises

32. Edwards, *Scientific and Philosophical Writings*, 215–16.

33. Locke, *Human Understanding*, 179. See chapter entitled, "Of Our Complex Ideas of Substances."

34. Locke, *Human Understanding*, 179.

from it; and that gravity is no way diverse from a principle by which matter acts on matter.

23. Because it is universally allowed that gravity depends immediately on the divine influence; and because it may be proved that solidity and gravity are in a good sense the same, and resolvable into each other; and because solidity has been proved to be the very being of a body: therefore we may infallibly conclude that the very being, and the manner of being, and the whole of bodies depends immediately on the divine power.[35]

It should be noted here that, just as *body, solidity, indivisibility, resistance,* and *motion* are attributed by Edwards to the immediate power of God, so too is *gravity:* "it is universally allowed," he insists, "that gravity depends immediately on the divine influence." It should also be noted, however, that this passage reveals a certain tension or ambivalence in Edwards's mind in this matter. On the one hand there is, on his part, a denial of mechanism—he refers to "that folly of seeking for a mechanical cause of gravity"; he also makes this observation: "therefore we may infallibly conclude that the very being, and the manner of being, and the whole of bodies depends immediately on the divine power." On the other hand, there is, on his part, an assertion of mechanism: "this has as much a mechanical cause as anything in the world, and is as philosophically to be solved, and ought no more to be attributed to the immediate operation of God than everything else."

THE NEWTONIAN REVOLUTION

Pivotal to our comprehension of Edwards's thought at this point is the fact that Edwards lived in a distinctly Newtonian universe. Newton's publication of his *Principia* in 1687 constitutes one of the great watersheds in intellectual history. Newton's three laws of motion, together with his law of universal gravitation, had a profound impact not only upon the scientific world, but also upon the religious world. Dudley Shapere comments that "the Newtonian theory came increasingly to favour deism and, eventually, a view of the universe as determined by inexorable laws. Mechanism thus became equated with determinism, and the Newtonian world picture came to be thought of as a picture of a Newtonian world machine."[36] "This deist God was himself," observes Crane Brinton, "a highly rationalistic construct—the 'clockmaker god' who had to exist in order to start this 'Newtonian

35. Edwards, *Scientific and Philosophical Writings*, 234–35.

36. Shapere, *Encyclopedia of Philosophy*, s.v. "Newton, Isaac."

world-machine' running, and guarantee that it would not run down, but who never interfered with it, and certainly never performed miracles."[37] Thus mechanics came to be regarded as the ultimate explanatory science, and it was believed that phenomena of any kind could and should be explained in terms of mechanical conceptions. The advent of Newtonian mechanics led before long, and in a manner totally unwanted, it seems, by its author, to a purely mechanistic physics. Elwood observes that "the new scientism ruled out the immediate activity of God in the world."[38]

There is, therefore, an inextricable connection between the Newtonian revolution and the rise of deism. It is very important to note that the central idea in deism was that God had, in the beginning, communicated self-subsistence and self-sustentation to the cosmos. God was construed as the Supreme Being—the great Architect or Mechanic who had created the universe in the beginning, but who then left the universe to run its own course as a self-operating machine. In other words, God had, supposedly, delegated all to second causes, subsequent to the initial creation. God was now, in deism, essentially an "absentee God." Newtonian science had, albeit unintentionally, led to what has been described, variously, as "the mathematization of nature"[39] or "the depersonalization of Providence."[40] Thus Edwards was responding to what Michael J. McClymond describes as "a growing tendency in eighteenth-century thought to marginalize God and remove God from significant involvement in nature, history, and human affairs."[41] "The chief problem of the eighteenth century," observes Elwood, "became one of relocating God in a post-Newtonian universe."[42]

37. Brinton, *Encyclopedia of Philosophy*, s.v. "Enlightenment."

38. Elwood, *Philosophical Theology*, 50.

39. Westfall, *Never at Rest*, 14.

40. Fiering, *Edwards's Moral Thought*, 93.

41. McClymond, *Encounters with God*, 80.

42. Elwood, *Philosophical Theology*, 51. Marsden, "Edwards in the Twenty-First Century," 154, makes this observation with regard to "the context in which Edwards was working." "In my view, it is especially important to view him as someone who was deeply loyal to the Puritan and wider Reformed or Calvinistic traditions of the seventeenth century and who was also informed by the Newtonian revolution and profoundly challenged by the British Enlightenment of his own era. One of the things that makes Edwards so interesting is that the Puritan side of him looks back to the Christendom of the Middle Ages and the Reformation, while the Newtonian and Enlightenment issues he was addressing look forward to the modern era. Facing the juxtaposition of these two vastly different outlooks so directly, he was acutely alert to some of the most significant implications of modernity."

MECHANISM

Edwards's observations on "mechanism" must, therefore, be understood in the context of the eighteenth century's preoccupation with the concept of autonomy, and this context explains the obvious ambivalence on Edwards's part with regard to mechanism. Mechanism is something that Edwards both affirms and denies—this is the startling paradox in Edwards's thought. He affirms mechanism in the sense that he ostensibly embraces the significance of "the new astronomy" and "the new science" with regard to the laws of nature; he denies it in the sense that he insists that the immediate power of God is the crucial factor in the laws of nature. Anderson expresses the paradox and the tension in Edwards's thought thus:

> Edwards himself, throughout his scientific writings, appears as an advocate of this new physics. He assumes that phenomena in nature are to be explained by the sizes, shapes, and motions of material particles, by the impulses and other forces that affect their motions, and the universal laws that govern them. He assumes a strictly deterministic universe in which every body affects every other according to those laws, and infers that God must have arranged the atoms with infinite care and wisdom in the first creation in order that all subsequent events, even miraculous ones, should follow according to the divine plan. In view of all this, his denial at the same time that matter is a real substance would have struck most of his informed contemporaries as paradoxical. Edwards's own statement . . . that "no matter is, in the most proper sense, matter," is a reflection of the paradox.[43]

This, then, is the question: Does Edwards believe in mechanism or not? If so, what exactly does mechanism mean for Edwards? Does his emphasis upon divine immediacy effectively preclude mechanism? What place is there, in Edwards's system, for natural law and secondary causes? Can mechanism and immediacy truly be reconciled in his system? It is obvious that Edwards denies mechanism in the deistic sense of the word. This fact emerges in "Of Atoms":

> *Corol. 16.* Hence there is no such thing as mechanism, if that word is taken to be that whereby bodies act each upon other, purely and properly by themselves.[44]

43. Edwards, *Scientific and Philosophical Writings*, 56.
44. Edwards, *Scientific and Philosophical Writings*, 216.

But the careful, guarded way in which Edwards expresses this conviction clearly implies that the word "mechanism" can be understood in another sense—a sense which emerges in the two preceding Corollaries:

> *Corol. 14.* We by this also clearly see that creation of the corporeal universe is nothing but the first causing resistance in such parts of space as God thought fit, with a power of being communicated successively from one part of space to another, according to such stated conditions as his infinite wisdom directed; and then the first beginning of this communication, so that ever after it might be continued without deviating from those stated conditions.
>
> *Corol. 15.* Hence we see what's that we call the laws of nature in bodies, to wit: the stated methods of God's acting with respect to bodies, and the stated conditions of the alteration of the manner of his acting.[45]

What is so significant here in these Corollaries is the way in which Edwards refers to the laws of nature: they are, quite simply, "the stated conditions"—"the stated methods of God's acting with respect to bodies, and the stated conditions of the alteration of the manner of his acting." Thus, according to Edwards, God acts via the laws of nature which he himself created, and he acts immediately via these laws. Edwards's concern here is not so much to deny the concept of "mechanism" and "the laws of nature" as to redefine these concepts and to qualify the general understanding of these terms. Negatively, he emphatically rejects the deistic concept of self-sustentation according to which "bodies act each upon other, purely and properly by themselves" and, positively, he emphatically insists upon a cosmology in which "the laws of nature in bodies" constitute, in fact, "the stated methods of God's acting." The problem here, however, is that Edwards appears to suggest that God operates immediately via the laws of nature—that he operates immediately via second causes—and it raises the specter of occasionalism.

THE QUESTION OF OCCASIONALISM

It is important that at this point we consider Edwards's observation in *Corollary 13* with regard to "divine concourse":

> *Corol. 13.* From all which, we find that what divines used to say concerning divine concourse had a great deal of truth lay at the bottom of it.[46]

45. Edwards, *Scientific and Philosophical Writings*, 216.

46. Edwards, *Scientific and Philosophical Writings*, 216.

Edwards acknowledges here the significance of the doctrine of *concursus* (a running together); indeed, he implicitly claims this position as his own. *Concursus* is defined by Louis Berkhof thus:

> Concurrence may be defined as the operation of the divine power with all subordinate powers, according to the pre-established laws of their operation, causing them to act and to act precisely as they do.[47]

Berkhof notes that this doctrine implies two things:

1. That the powers of nature do not work by themselves, that is, simply by their own inherent power, but that God is immediately operative in every act of the creature. This must be maintained in opposition to the deistic position.
2. That second causes are real, and not to be regarded simply as the operative power of God. It is only on condition that second causes are real, that we can properly speak of a concurrence or cooperation of the First Cause with secondary causes. This should be stressed over against the pantheistic idea that God is the only agent working in the world.[48]

It is evident that the doctrine of *concursus*, as defined by Berkhof here, seeks to steer a *via media* (middle way) between the deistic position, which denies any immediate involvement on the part of God, and the pantheistic position, which denies the reality of secondary causes. Indeed, the concept of *concursus* is pivotal to the classic theistic position which posits a conjunction of first and second causes in the preservation of the cosmos. But is Edwards's position here really that of *concursus*? His emphasis upon the immediacy of God clearly precludes deism, but does it preclude pantheism? Can Edwards legitimately claim that "second causes are real, and not to be regarded simply as the operative power of God"? The fundamental problem here is that of Edwards's juxtaposition of immediacy on the one hand and mechanism on the other. The question, basically, is this: How can there be a *concursus* between immediacy and means? If the immediacy is genuine and pure, then means are no more means; and if the means are genuine and pure, then immediacy is no more immediacy. This, then, is the problem: How can Edwards insist, at one and the same time, upon immediacy and mechanism? The inevitable tendency of the one is ever that of suppressing the other, and such is Edwards's enormous insistence upon immediacy that, in his system, mechanism tends to be suppressed. The immediacy of

47. Berkhof, *Systematic Theology*, 171.

48. Berkhof, *Systematic Theology*, 171–72.

the First Cause appears to swallow up the efficacy and the reality of second causes. In short, the specter of occasionalism remains.

CONTINUOUS CREATION

Moreover, the specter of occasionalism as a fundamental aspect of Edwards's thought intensifies when we consider what must surely rank as the most remarkable expression of Edwards's concept of divine immediacy; namely, his doctrine of continuous creation. If Edwards's endorsement of the Augustinian-Boethian position with regard to the atemporality of God reflects his emphasis upon the immediacy of God's knowledge, his endorsement of the doctrine of continuous creation reflects his emphasis upon the immediacy of God's power. The *locus classicus* (classic place) for this particular doctrine is to be found towards the close of his treatise, *The Great Christian Doctrine of Original Sin Defended* (1758). At this point in the treatise Edwards is concerned to refute "that great objection against the imputation of Adam's sin to his posterity considered, that such imputation is unjust and unreasonable, inasmuch as Adam and his posterity are not one and the same."[49] Edwards answers this objection by making a metaphysical claim about identity and, in particular, about identity through time.[50] His argument here is essentially analogical. He contends that, just as in the realm of biblical anthropology the oneness or identity of Adam and his posterity is established by "divine constitution,"[51] so in the realm of creation the oneness or identity of individuals persisting through time is established by "God's sovereign constitution."[52] Pivotal to Edwards's argument here is his extraordinary doctrine of continuous creation.

At this point in his treatise, Edwards engages in what Helm has described as "a metaphysical excursus"[53]—an excursus in which the Stockbridge philosopher-theologian utilizes "a version of the doctrine of temporal parts."[54] But the radical nature of Edwards's argument here does not emerge immediately:

> God not only created all things, and gave them being at first, but continually preserves them, and upholds them in being. This

49. Edwards, *Original Sin*, 389.
50. See Helm, *Faith and Understanding*, 154.
51. Edwards, *Original Sin*, 404.
52. Edwards, *Original Sin*, 399.
53. Helm, *Faith and Understanding*, 161.
54. Helm, *Faith and Understanding*, 157.

> being a matter of considerable importance, it may be worthy here to be considered with a little attention. Let us inquire therefore, in the first place, whether it ben't [*sic*] evident, that God does continually, by his immediate power, uphold every created substance in being; and then let us see the consequence.[55]

At this stage in his argument, Edwards appears simply to be endorsing the traditional theistic concept of divine upholding or divine preservation, although it should be noted that there is, even here, a strong emphasis upon God's "immediate power." Thus it is an immediate upholding and preservation on God's part that Edwards endorses. Edwards is clearly concerned to refute here the position of the deists who held that God had, in the beginning, communicated self-subsistence or self-sustentation to the cosmos. Indeed, this concept of the self-subsistence or the self-sustentation of the creation constitutes the central idea in deism. It should be noted that, when Edwards refutes the notion that the "antecedent existence" of the moon is the cause of its "present existence," he is refuting an essentially deistic notion. The cause of the moon's "present existence," Edwards insists, does not lie in its "past existence"; it lies in the immediate power of the Creator.

But what Helm describes as "his anti-deistic impulse,"[56] "his anti-deistic impetus,"[57] is not yet fully spent. Indeed, it constrains Edwards to embrace a more radical position:

> If any shall . . . insist upon it, that there is no need of any immediate divine power, to produce the present existence of created substances, but that their present existence is the effect or consequence of past existence, according to the nature of things; that the established course of nature is sufficient to continue existence, where existence is once given; I allow it: but then it should be remembered, what nature is, in created things; and what the established course of nature is; that, as has been observed already, it is nothing, separate from the agency of God; and that, as Dr. Taylor says, "God, the Original of all being, is the only cause of all natural effects." A father, according to the course of nature, begets a child; an oak, according to the course of nature, produces an acorn, or a bud; so according to the course of nature, the former existence of the trunk of the tree is followed by its new or present existence. In the one case, and the other, the new effect is consequent on the former, only by the established laws, and settled course of nature; which is

55. Edwards, *Original Sin*, 400.
56. Helm, "Forensic Dilemma," 54.
57. Helm, "Forensic Dilemma," 50.

> allowed to be nothing but the continued immediate efficiency of God, according to a constitution that he has been pleased to establish. Therefore, as our author greatly urges, that the child and the acorn, which come into existence according to the course of nature, in consequence of the prior existence and state of the parent and the oak, are truly *immediately* created or made by God; so must the existence of each created person and thing, at each moment of it, be from the immediate *continued* creation of God. It will certainly follow from these things, that God's *preserving* created things in being is perfectly equivalent to a *continued creation,* or to his creating those things out of nothing at *each moment* of their existence. If the continued existence of created things be wholly dependent on God's preservation, then those things would drop into nothing, upon the ceasing of the present moment, without a new exertion of the divine power to cause them to exist in the following moment.[58]

It now emerges that Edwards is insisting here not only that the cause of the moon's "present existence" does not lie in its "past existence," but also that it does not even lie in the fact of God's preservation; it lies rather in the fact that God continuously re-creates the moon *ex nihilo* (from nothing) at every successive moment. Thus the radical twist that Edwards imparts here to his otherwise theistic position is that of an unashamed assertion of the doctrine of continuous creation. "It will certainly follow from these things, that God's preserving created things in being is perfectly equivalent to a continued creation, or to his creating those things out of nothing at each moment of their existence." It now becomes apparent, as he develops his argument, that Edwards believes not only in an original *creatio ex nihilo* (creation out of nothing) and in the immediate preservation of that creation, but also in *creatio continua* and thus, by definition, in an almost infinite series of *creationes ex nihilo* (creations out of nothing). Indeed, any difference that might conceivably pertain between the original *creatio ex nihilo* in the beginning and the series of *creationes ex nihilo* at every successive moment since is, Edwards contends, purely circumstantial:

> It will follow from what has been observed, that God's upholding of created substance, or causing of its existence in each successive moment, is altogether equivalent to an *immediate production out of nothing,* at each moment, because its existence at this moment is not merely in part from God, but wholly from him; and not in any part, or degree, from its antecedent existence. For the supposing that its antecedent existence *concurs* with

58. Edwards, *Original Sin*, 401–2.

> God in *efficiency*, to produce some part of the effect, is attended with all the very same absurdities, which have been shown to attend the supposition of its producing it wholly. Therefore the antecedent existence is nothing, as to any proper influence or assistance in the affair: and consequently God produces the effect as much from *nothing*, as if there had been nothing *before*. So that this effect differs not at all from the first creation, but only *circumstantially*.[59]

There is, interestingly, a certain oscillation here on Edwards's part between two different doctrines on divine creation, identity, and time. According to the weaker doctrine, the sun, the moon, and the stars (for instance) will not continue to exist for a moment longer unless God wills their continued existence—this is the doctrine of divine upholding or preservation. According to the stronger doctrine, the sun, the moon, and the stars will not continue to exist for a moment longer unless God re-creates them for that moment, and continues to re-create them for all succeeding moments of their existence—this is the doctrine of continuous creation. It is very important to note that the weaker thesis is insufficient to establish Edwards's desired conclusion in his adducing of this analogy—the desired conclusion requires the stronger thesis of *creatio continua* and its corollary—the doctrine of temporal parts. In view of the fact that the very purpose of the adducing of this analogy in *Original Sin* is the establishment of the concept of the oneness or identity of Adam and his posterity, the conclusion must be deemed incontrovertible that Edwards commits himself here to the stronger doctrine of *creatio continua*.[60]

It now becomes apparent that not only does Edwards attribute *body, solidity, indivisibility, resistance, motion*, and *gravity* to the immediate power of God, but also *existence itself*—that is to say, the continued, moment-by-moment existence of the universe itself. These spheres are obviously inextricably related and they logically cohere. If we grant *creatio continua*, then, *a fortiori* (all the more/how much more), the lesser spheres inevitably follow. The question that arises, therefore, is this: Does Edwards formally teach *creatio continua* elsewhere in his writings? In short, is this doctrine of continuous creation a consistent strand in his philosophy and his theology, or might it be deemed simply a late philosophical-theological aberration on his part?

We note at this point the significance of two relatively early *Miscellanies*, both of which precede the crucial passage in *Original Sin* by some thirty years:

59. Edwards, *Original Sin*, 402.

60. I am indebted, in this paragraph, to Helm, "Forensic Dilemma," 55.

> Miscellany 125. GOD'S EXISTENCE. 'Tis certain with me that the world exists anew every moment, that the existence of things every moment ceases and is every moment renewed.[61]

This Miscellany was, according to Thomas A. Schafer, written during Edwards's Yale tutorship in July or August 1725.[62] The following Miscellany was written at least three years later at some point between July 1728 and February 1729.[63] By now Edwards was preaching regularly in the church at Northampton.

> Miscellany 346. CREATION. PROVIDENCE. It [is] most agreeable to the Scripture, to suppose creation to be performed new every moment.[64]

The evidence of these two Miscellanies demonstrates overwhelmingly that the concept of continuous creation was not, in fact, some temporary aberration on Edwards's part, imported by him into the treatise on *Original Sin*, only to be jettisoned by him at other times; rather, it was clearly a conviction consistently held by him from the beginning of his intellectual career. It is very important to note that Edwards articulated this extraordinary doctrine of *creatio continua* both at the outset and at the close of his career, and, it must be presumed, was convinced of its truth throughout the years that intervened. Indeed, as *Miscellany 346* demonstrates, Edwards believed, perhaps unreasonably, that this doctrine was taught by the Scriptures themselves. This fact, in turn, has very important consequences; namely, that, if there is, in his system, any tension between this strand and other strands, those other strands will surely need to be adjusted to this, rather than *vice versa*.

THE DEIST'S POSITION

It is interesting to note that, in Edwards's discussion of creation in this passage in *Original Sin*, it is possible to identify three distinct positions, whether rejected, considered, or espoused. Firstly, there is the *deistic* position. This position asserts that God is the First Cause and that, as such, he created the great cosmic clock in the beginning and now simply leaves it to run according to secondary laws. God is, in effect, a mere distant and passive spectator of the world and of its operations and exerts no direct efficiency

61. Edwards, *Miscellanies*, 288.
62. Edwards, *Miscellanies*, 156.
63. Edwards, *Miscellanies*, 157.
64. Edwards, *Miscellanies*, 418.

in sustaining the things which he has made. The creation is not dependent upon the Creator for its continuing existence. Indeed, God's preservation of the cosmos is reduced by the deists to an *actus negativus* (a negative act) whereby God simply refrains from destroying the cosmos. Thus, according to this position, the present existence of the moon, for instance, is to be explained by its prior, antecedent existence. The original creation of the moon supposedly accounts for its present existence and, indeed, its future existence. The divine preservation of the moon is simply unnecessary—much less the continuous creation of the moon at every successive moment. W.G.T. Shedd explains thus "the deistical view of providence"[65]:

> God is not immediately present nor does he operate directly, but only at a distance. This amounts to communicating self-subsistence to the creature. God so constitutes the creation that it can continue to exist and move by means of its own inherent properties and laws . . . The deistical theory, consequently, implies that matter, after its creation, is self-sustaining and self-governing.[66]

It should be noted that Edwards specifically rejects this deistical notion in the following passage:

> For instance, the existence of the body of the moon at this present moment, can't be the effect of its existence at the last foregoing moment. For not only was what existed the last moment, no active cause, but wholly a passive thing; but this also is to be considered, that no cause can produce effects in a *time* and *place* on which itself is *not*. 'Tis plain, nothing can exert itself, or operate, when and where it is not existing. But the moon's past existence was neither *where* nor *when* its present existence is.[67]

THE THEIST'S POSITION

Secondly, there is the *theistic* position. This position asserts that God is the First Cause, but that, in contradistinction to the deistic view, he is also the Sustainer of the universe. Thus, according to this position, the present existence of the moon is to be explained, not simply by virtue of its antecedent existence, but by virtue of God's continually upholding or preserving it by his power. Against deism, the theistic position denies the concept of the

65. Shedd, *Dogmatic Theology*, 1.528.
66. Shedd, *Dogmatic Theology*, 1.528.
67. Edwards, *Scientific and Philosophical Writings*, 400.

self-subsistence or the self-sustentation of the moon and insists upon the constant activity of God in its preservation. The creation is dependent upon the Creator for its preservation:

> God not only created all things, and gave them being at first, but continually preserves them, and upholds them in being . . . Let us inquire therefore, in the first place, whether it ben't evident, that God does continually, by his immediate power, uphold every created substance in being.[68]

This is the position that Edwards appears initially to endorse in this passage—it is, of course, the classic, traditional Christian position. But the question with which Edwards appears to be consumed is this: Is this theistic position of divine upholding or preservation sufficiently powerful as a counterblast to deism? Moreover, is it sufficiently powerful to establish the concept of an arbitrary divine constitution of Adam's progeny as one? The answer that Edwards gives would appear to be in the negative on both counts.

EDWARDS'S POSITION

> So must the existence of each created person and thing, at each moment of it, be from the immediate *continued* creation of God. It will certainly follow from these things, that God's *preserving* of created things in being is perfectly equivalent to a *continued creation,* or to his creating those things out of nothing at *each moment* of their existence. If the continued existence of created things be wholly dependent on God's preservation, then those things would drop into nothing, upon the ceasing of the present moment, without a new exertion of the divine power to cause them to exist in the following moment.[69]

This is clearly a much stronger, more radical position than the theistic position. The creation is dependent at every successive moment upon the Creator, not only for its preservation, but even for its very existence. Moreover, it is this stronger, more radical position that is required by the daring analogy that Edwards is seeking to establish at this point in his argument. That analogy is, supposedly, between the oneness and identity of the temporal parts or the temporal slices implicit in the concept of continuous

68. Edwards, *Scientific and Philosophical Writings*, 400.

69. Edwards, *Scientific and Philosophical Writings*, 401–02.

creation on the one hand and the oneness and identity between Adam and his posterity on the other. Edwards's argument is that, in each element of the analogy, although the individual parts are *not* one, but a series, God "treats them as one."[70] In each case the identity or oneness depends, Edwards contends, on "God's sovereign constitution"[71] or "the arbitrary constitution of the Creator."[72]

THE DOCTRINE OF TEMPORAL PARTS

Oliver D. Crisp explains thus the inextricable connection between a doctrine of continuous creation and a doctrine of temporal parts:

> This is the view according to which God creates the world out of nothing, whereupon it momentarily ceases to exist, to be replaced by a facsimile that has incremental differences built into it to account for what appears to be motion and change across time. This, in turn is annihilated, or ceases to exist, and is replaced by another facsimile world that has incremental differences built into it to account for what appear to be motion and change across time, and so on.[73]

Crisp provides the following helpful analogy to illustrate this doctrine of temporal parts:

> An analogy with a motion picture may help to make this doctrine clearer to a modern readership. When watching a movie at the cinema we appear to see a sequence of actions across time represented in the projected images on the silver screen. But in reality, the images are a reel of photographic stills run together at speed to give the illusion of motion and action across time. Similarly with the doctrine of continuous creation: the world seems to persist through time, but in fact it does not. "The world" (meaning here, the created cosmos) is merely shorthand for that series of created "stills"—that is, the complete, maximal, but momentary states of affairs—God brings about in sequence, playing, as it were, on the silver screen of the divine mind.[74]

70. Edwards, *Scientific and Philosophical Writings*, 403.
71. Edwards, *Scientific and Philosophical Writings*, 404.
72. Edwards, *Scientific and Philosophical Writings*, 403.
73. Crisp, *God and Creation*, 25.
74. Crisp, *God and Creation*, 25–26.

It is important to note that a doctrine of temporal parts is the inevitable corollary of Edwards's concept of continuous creation. The value of this analogy of a motion picture lies in the fact that it combines the concept of continuous activity with the concept of settled stability.

SANG HYUN LEE

It is, at this stage, important to consider Sang Hyun Lee's assessment of Edwards's putative occasionalism. Lee effectively exonerates Edwards from the charge of occasionalism:

> It will be recalled that Edwards asserted in an early note in "Natural Philosophy" that "the universe is created out of nothing every moment." This still obtains in the sense that it is God who constantly preserves the established general laws *and* causes actual existences according to those laws. But it is not a continual *creatio ex nihilo* in a simple sense. The divinely established general laws are given a permanence, and are in a sense not created ex nihilo every moment. Edwards's view is an occasionalism only in the sense that God moves the world from virtuality to full actuality every moment through an immediate exercise of his power. Edwards's view is not an unqualified occasionalist position, however, since the world has an abiding reality in a virtual mode.[75]
>
> In this way, Edwards maintains a balance between God's direct and continual involvement in the created world's actual existence, on the one hand, and the created world's relative and yet real contribution to its actuality, on the other. In other words, Edwards avoids deism as well as occasionalism. God's direct involvement precludes deism, and Edwards avoids occasionalism because God's continuous creative activity is in accordance with his preestablished and abiding laws.[76]

We concede that Edwards avoids deism; we are not so sanguine that Edwards avoids occasionalism. After all, it is Lee himself who, in referring to "the occasionalist doctrine that God, the only causal power, creates the world *ex nihilo* from moment to moment"[77] defines occasionalism in the very terms used by Edwards himself in defining *creatio continua* in *Original Sin*. Lee does not, in our judgment, deal adequately with the crucial

75. Lee, *Philosophical Theology*, 63.
76. Lee, *Philosophical Theology*, 107.
77. Lee, *Philosophical Theology*, 71.

passage in *Original Sin*—in fact, remarkably, he does not deal with it at all.[78] Lee limits his consideration of this issue to Edwards's early philosophical writings and to the *Miscellanies;* he has neglected, it seems, the *locus classicus* with regard to continuous creation and has, as a result, significantly underestimated Edwards's occasionalism. The problem here is that Lee has effectively reduced Edwards's doctrine of continuous creation to a doctrine of immediate preservation.

Lee's underestimation of Edwards's doctrine of *creatio continua* and of the resultant occasionalism in Edwards's system has, inevitably, significant ramifications with regard to his own philosophical-theological system. In his interpretation of Edwards's thought, Lee espouses what he describes as a "dispositional ontology"[79] in which the created order is to be understood in terms of dispositions, habits, or laws: "The created world," Lee insists, "is a network of divinely established habits and dispositions (or the so-called laws of nature)."[80] "Habits and laws, Edwards is saying, are the abiding principles of being."[81] Indeed, Lee regards Edwards's category of disposition or habits as "the interpretive key"[82] to Edwards's thought. Lee's position has, according to Crisp, become "the dominant interpretation of Jonathan Edwards's philosophical theology."[83]

The problem here, however, is that the very concept of disposition, habit, and law (as applied by Lee) implies the concept of the continuity of created existence, for these terms express the properties of a continuing object. Edwards's doctrine of continuous creation, however, clearly precludes such a concept. For Edwards, there is no continuity inherent in created existence; rather, created existence consists, he contends, of an infinite number of temporal parts or temporal slices that are segued together by God in such a manner as to produce the apparent effect of persistence through time. Thus the alleged permanence of the created order, upon which Lee insists, is, strictly speaking, an illusion. Crisp makes the following observations with regard to Lee's interpretation: "The dispositions and habits that constitute creatures (in his interpretation of Edwards) were momentary in nature, coming into existence only to be immediately annihilated and replaced by

78. It is a remarkable fact that Lee's work, *The Philosophical Theology of Jonathan Edwards*, contains only three specific references to Original Sin. See op. cit., 41, 44, 142. None of these references deals with the pivotal doctrine of continuous creation.

79. Lee, *Philosophical Theology*, 48.

80. Lee, *Philosophical Theology*, 8.

81. Lee, *Philosophical Theology*, 48.

82. Lee, *Philosophical Theology*, 7.

83. Crisp, *God and Creation*, 14.

numerically distinct facsimiles, seriatim";[84] "there are no laws that persist through time independent of divine fiat."[85] Certainly, it is important to acknowledge that, while there is, in a very real sense, a radical contingence about the creation, this radical contingence, since it is in the hands of God, should not be construed as indicating chaos, uncertainty, or instability, but is, in Edwards's mind, perfectly compatible with stability, regularity, and order. Thus it can be conceded that Lee's insistence upon the permanence of the created realm does possess a certain *prima facie* plausibility; there is, indeed, an apparent permanence to the created order. Nevertheless, in the final analysis Edwards's radical insistence upon the immediacy of God, the supreme expression of which is, surely, his doctrine of continuous creation, proves to be powerfully subversive of Lee's position concerning habit or disposition.

NICOLAS MALEBRANCHE (1638–1715)

Edwards's occasionalism, which is surely the inevitable corollary of his doctrine of *creatio continua,* appears to derive primarily from the French philosopher-priest, Nicolas Malebranche (1638–1715). In 1675, Malebranche, the father of the occasionalist philosophy, published *De la recherche de la vérité.*[86] In this work, he expresses his fundamental position thus: "There is only one true cause because there is only one true God; that the nature or power of each thing is nothing but the will of God; that all natural causes are not *true* causes but only *occasional* causes."[87]

> For if religion teaches us that there is only one true God, this philosophy shows us that there is only one true cause. If religion teaches us that all the divinities of paganism are merely stones and metals without life or motion, this philosophy also reveals to us that all secondary causes, or all the divinities of philosophy, are merely matter and inefficacious wills. Finally, if religion teaches us that we must not genuflect before false gods, this philosophy also teaches us that our imaginations and minds must not bow before the imaginary greatness and power

84. Crisp, *God and Creation*, 36.

85. Crisp, *God and Creation*, 29.

86. Steven Nadler makes the following observation with regard to this work: "The Search represents a grand synthesis of the systems of Malebranche's two intellectual (and spiritual) mentors, Augustine and Descartes." Nadler, *Cambridge Companion to Malebranche*, 3.

87. Lennon and Olskamp, *Search after Truth*, 448.

> of causes that are not causes at all; that we must neither love nor fear them; that we must not be concerned with them; that we must think only of God alone, see God in all things, fear and love God in all things.[88]

Thus, for Malebranche, "bodies themselves are inefficacious"[89]—"God is the true cause of motion in bodies."[90] He adds:

> Accordingly, when one ball strikes a second ball and the second ball moves, God is the real or true cause . . . of the second ball's moving. Since he acts, not at random, but in accordance with general laws of motion that he has enacted, the impact of the first ball may be called the occasional, or particular, cause . . . of the second ball's moving.[91]

It is evident from the general tenor of this passage that Malebranche regarded the notion of second causes as idolatrous and blasphemous. As far as Malebranche was concerned, God, "the Author of all motion in matter,"[92] is directly, immediately, and solely responsible for bringing about all phenomena.

Malebranche was, of course, reacting vigorously to the metaphysical materialism of his day. The cardinal tenet of the materialistic philosophy is defined by Keith Campbell thus: "Everything that is, is material."[93] "Therefore, there are no incorporeal souls or spirits, no spiritual principalities or powers, no angels or devils, no demiurges and no gods (if these are conceived as immaterial entities). Hence, nothing that happens can be attributed to the action of such beings."[94] The second major tenet of materialism is defined by Campbell thus: "Everything that can be explained can be explained on the basis of laws involving only the antecedent physical conditions."[95] Thus, historically, materialists have tended to be determinists. Anderson makes this observation concerning the world into which Edwards was born:

> It was generally conceded that bodies sustain and transmit motion to each other by themselves, without the operation of immaterial causes, according to fixed mathematical and

88. Lennon and Olskamp, *Search after Truth*, 452.
89. Doney, *Encyclopedia of Philosophy*, s.v. "Malebranche, Nicolas."
90. Doney, *Encyclopedia of Philosophy*, s.v. "Malebranche, Nicolas."
91. Doney, *Encyclopedia of Philosophy*, s.v. "Malebranche, Nicolas."
92. Lennon and Olskamp, *Search after Truth*, 225.
93. Campbell, *Encyclopedia of Philosophy*, s.v. "materialism."
94. Campbell, *Encyclopedia of Philosophy*, s.v. "materialism."
95. Campbell, *Encyclopedia of Philosophy*, s.v. "materialism."

> mechanical laws; and that the purely physical world can thus be conceived as an entirely autonomous, self-sustaining, and deterministic system.[96]

> Materialism proposed that the universe is a complete, autonomous, and self-sustaining system of unthinking bodies that are subject only to inherent, necessary, and mathematically exact laws of mechanical causation; and so it ruled out the conception of a divine and providential government of the world.[97]

Malebranche's anti-materialist, occasionalist *Weltanschauung* is clearly well established. But what, if any, was Edwards's intellectual contact with Malebranche? It is at this point that we note the crucial significance of the Dummer gift of books to Yale College in 1714. Jeremiah Dummer was a colonial agent whose collection of books constituted, according to Fiering, "a massive updating of Yale's then meager resources."[98] Peter J. Thuesen makes this observation with regard to the Dummer gift:

> Though the books were donated in 1714, they were not accessible until Edwards's senior year, by which time the college had been consolidated in New Haven. Edwards would have had the opportunity to use the new library during his years as a master's degree candidate (1720–22) and a tutor (1724–26). Indeed, Edwards and the other tutors received an extra stipend for sorting the books, which Dummer had collected from individual donors, many of them prominent figures . . . The collection also featured . . . Nicolas Malebranche's *Search After Truth*.[99]

Thuesen further remarks that "Edwards was also aware of the English edition of *The Search after Truth* . . ., as well as works by Malebranche's English followers John Norris . . . and Arthur Collier."[100] It is important to note that Edwards's *Catalogue of Books* contains a number of references to Malebranche's works. Thus it is evident that Malebranche's major work was available and accessible to the Yale student, that Malebranche constituted a significant element in Edwards's world of books, and that it is almost certain that Edwards had read Malebranche's *Search after Truth*, probably in English translation. What Stephen H. Daniel has termed "the Malebranche-Edwards

96. Edwards, *Scientific and Philosophical Writings*, 55–56.

97. Edwards, *Scientific and Philosophical Writings*, 54.

98. Fiering, *Jonathan Edwards's Moral Thought*, 22.

99. Edwards, *Catalogue of Books*, 9–10.

100. Edwards, *Catalogue of Books*, 91.

connection"[101] is clearly well established. The evidence is overwhelming that Edwards's occasionalist tendencies derive essentially from Nicolas Malebranche. Indeed, it is highly probable that the youthful Edwards was one of the first on the North American continent to be confronted by Malebranche's thought.

It will be noted immediately that, in its extreme theocentrism, the *malebranchiste* philosophy effectively involves a denial of the reality and the integrity of second causes: "This philosophy," Malebranche insists, "also reveals to us that all secondary causes, or all the divinities of philosophy, are merely matter and inefficacious wills." But is this Edwards's position? His statement that "there is no such thing as mechanism, if that word is taken to be that whereby bodies act each upon other, purely and properly by themselves"; his reference to "what's that we call the laws of nature in bodies, to wit: the stated methods of God's acting with respect to bodies"; his view that body, solidity, indivisibility, resistance, motion, gravity, and existence itself are to be understood as manifestations of the immediate power of God—these positions are clearly perfectly consistent with occasionalism. Moreover, is it not the case that Edwards's extraordinary doctrine of *creatio continua* necessarily requires an occasionalist philosophy? Certainly, Edwards is not as overt as Malebranche in the assertion of an occasionalist philosophy; but is not such a philosophy the logical conclusion of the doctrine of continuous creation? If all things throughout the universe are being re-created *ex nihilo* at every successive moment, as Edwards unashamedly insists in *Original Sin*, then there can surely be, from the standpoint of logic, no mundane causation and thus no place for second causes. Nothing is mediate; all is immediate. Just as there is, strictly speaking, no such thing as mechanism, so there is also no such thing as causes; there are only effects. The continuous activity of the First Cause in re-creating the universe *ex nihilo* at every successive moment effectively precludes and excludes second causes. Some form of occasionalism is, surely, the inevitable corollary of a doctrine of continuous creation.

THE LAWS OF NATURE

Thus in Edwards's occasionalistic approach to the laws of nature we note the remarkable predictabilities and regularities in the functioning of the cosmos—we note the law-likeness which marks its functioning in general. But the laws, as such, do not constitute the *sine qua non* (without which there is not) of the functioning of the cosmos; rather, the cosmos operates

101. Daniel, "Edwards' Occasionalism," 1.

via the immediate power of the Creator. It is the immediate power of God that constitutes the *sine qua non* of the operation of the cosmos—the laws themselves simply describe or reflect the circumstances in which God's immediate activity operates. It should be noted that there is, on Edwards's part, no formal denial of the concept of physical law; indeed, in the pivotal passage in *Original Sin*, he explicitly endorses the concept of "the course of nature." His reference to "the established laws and settled course of nature" demonstrates that he acknowledges the *prima facie* reality of the concept of natural, physical law. He insists, however, that "the established course of nature" is "nothing separate from the agency of God," that "the established laws and settled course of nature" are "nothing but the continued immediate efficiency of God."[102] Thus, while there is, on Edwards's part, no formal, explicit denial of the concept of the laws of nature, there is a definite suppression of the concept of natural law or second causes. Thomas A. Schafer expresses this truth thus:

> There simply is no realm of even relatively autonomous "second causes" between God and the world. Not only humankind but also all creation is immediately, totally dependent each moment on God's decision to continue both the fact and the manner of its existence. There are, of course, "natural laws" by which the world continues to operate; but what we call natural law is only the "method" or "rule" by which God has chosen to exercise his power.[103]

Thus laws such as the law of gravity are but the "stated conditions"—"the stated methods of God's acting." The course of nature with its established laws is effectively reduced in Edwards's system to the immediate agency of God. It would appear at this point to be incontrovertible that, with regard to the operation of the cosmos, Edwards views natural law as descriptive rather than as prescriptive—for Edwards natural law does not prescribe, but describes, the functioning of the universe. Crisp summarizes Edwards's position thus: "God occasionalistically 'conserves' the world commensurate with the appearance of there being physical laws that persist through time."[104] "Creatures are merely the occasions of God's action."[105]

Traditionally, Christian theology has, of course, always sought to steer a *via media* between deism on the one hand and pantheism on the other. In other words, it has always sought to steer a *via media* between an exaggerated

102. Edwards, *Original Sin*, 401.

103. Edwards, *Miscellanies a-500*, 42.

104. Crisp, *God and Creation*, 30.

105. Crisp, *Among the Theologians*, 166.

emphasis on God's transcendence (at the expense of his immanence) and an exaggerated emphasis upon God's immanence (at the expense of his transcendence). This *via media,* or the position of Christian theism, has sought to maintain, in tension and in balance, both God's absolute transcendence *above* the universe and his immanence *in* the universe. Certainly, it must be conceded that, within the general parameters of this *via media,* there are nuanced differences in the spectrum of Christian theism contingent upon the emphasis given now to transcendence, now to immanence. Where, precisely, then, does Edwards himself stand in this spectrum? It is surely incontestable that, in his massive emphasis upon the immediacy of God vis-à-vis the universe, in his apparently unashamed assertion of continuous creation in *Original Sin,* and in the occasionalism that is its inevitable corollary, Edwards must be deemed to stand at the extreme wing of Christian theism, on the very borderline between theism and pantheism. Indeed, he gives every impression of being dissatisfied with the traditional adjustment in Christian theology between God's transcendence and God's immanence. Thus, if deism be said to constitute the left wing, and pantheism the right wing, with theism in the center, then Edwards could be said to be often straining towards the extreme right wing of Christian theism, almost as if he were powerfully attracted by a monistic world-view.

THE PROBLEM OF INFINITY

Pivotal to an understanding of Edwards's apparent attraction to a monistic, pantheistic *Weltanschauung* is what might be termed "the problem of infinity." This problem inevitably arises in any philosophical-theological consideration of the relationship between God and the universe. The fundamental issue is this: Does the infinity of God include or exclude the finite—more precisely, does the infinite Creator include or exclude the finite creation? If we reply that the infinity of God excludes the finite, then this implies that it is possible to add to the infinite—in short, that the infinite is less than infinite; but if we reply that the infinity of God includes the finite, then this necessarily involves a position that is pantheizing in tendency. How is it possible, logically, to maintain the concept of the absolute infinity of God without conceding pantheism or, at the very least, panentheism? Keith Ward describes the general trends or tendencies in this matter thus: "Two contrasting models of God have dominated the history of philosophical theology . . . The two models . . . may be distinguished by their differing interpretations of the idea of 'infinity.'"[106] One model, notes Ward, is that of

106. Ward, *Rational Theology*, 1.

"the tradition of 'exclusive infinity.'"[107] According to this model the infinite God excludes all finite things from himself. This is, of course, the position held by traditional Christian theism. The other model is that of "the tradition of 'inclusive infinity.'"[108] In this model, God is understood as including all possible and actual things within himself, as in the various pantheizing traditions. Thus the universe is construed as an expression or emanation of the unlimited reality of God.

Don Schweitzer, for his part, notes the attributes basic to Edwards's understanding of God as infinite. The first attribute is what Schweitzer calls "the trajectory of qualitative difference between God and finite creation."[109] This trajectory coheres, of course, with Ward's concept of "exclusive infinity." The second attribute is that of "the trajectory of continuity between the finite and the infinite."[110] This trajectory coheres with Ward's concept of "inclusive infinity." The third attribute is that of "the comprehensiveness of God as infinite."[111] Schweitzer observes that this third attribute "puts these two trajectories into tension."[112] It is precisely this tension that one constantly notes in Edwards's philosophical theology; but it is a tension that, via his commitment to divine immediacy, constantly lures him in the direction of the concepts of "continuity" and "inclusive infinity." In Miscellany 697, written at some point in the mid-1730s, Edwards expresses himself thus:[113]

> Infinity and omneity, if I may so speak, must go together, because if any being falls short of omneity, then it is not infinite therein; it is limity [*sic*] therein; there is something that it don't extend to, or that it don't comprehend . . . An infinite being, therefore, must be an all-comprehending being. He must comprehend in himself all being . . . God—as he is infinite, and the being whence all are derived, and from whom every thing is given—does comprehend the entity of all his creatures; and their entity is not to be added to his, as not comprehended in it, for they are but communications from him.[114]

107. Ward, *Rational Theology*, 2.

108. Ward, *Rational Theology*, 2.

109. Schweitzer, "Understanding of Divine Infinity," 53.

110. Schweitzer, "Understanding of Divine Infinity," 53.

111. Schweitzer, "Understanding of Divine Infinity." 53.

112. Schweitzer, "Understanding of Divine Infinity," 53.

113. Ava Chamberlain provides helpful data with regard to the approximate date of Miscellany 697. See Edwards, *Miscellanies*, 501–832, 42–48.

114. Edwards, *Miscellanies*, 501–832, 281–82.

THE QUESTION OF PANENTHEISM

This apparent attraction to a monistic world-view on Edwards's part emerges supremely in *God's Chief End in Creation.* In this treatise, Edwards analyzes the issue of God's ultimate purpose in creating the universe. The following passages capture the essence of Edwards's position:

> As there is an infinite fulness of all possible good in God, a fulness of every perfection, of all excellency and beauty, and of infinite happiness. And as this fulness is capable of communication or emanation *ad extra;* so it seems a thing amiable and valuable in itself that it should be communicated or flow forth, that this infinite fountain of good should send forth abundant streams, that this infinite fountain of light should, diffusing its excellent fullness, pour forth light all around. And as this is in itself excellent, so a disposition to this in the Divine Being must be looked upon as an excellent disposition; such an emanation of good is, in some sense, a multiplication of it; so far as the communication or external stream may be looked upon as anything besides the fountain, so far it may be looked on as an increase of good. And if the fullness of good that is in the fountain is in itself excellent and worthy to exist, then the emanation, or that which is as it were an increase, repetition, or multiplication of it, is excellent and worthy to exist. Thus it is fit, since there is an infinite fountain of light and knowledge, that this light should shine forth in beams of communicated knowledge and understanding; and as there is an infinite fountain of holiness, moral excellence and beauty, so it should flow out in communicated holiness. And that as there is an infinite fullness of joy and happiness, so these should have an emanation, and become a fountain flowing out in abundant streams, as beams from the sun.[115]

Edwards then proceeds to summarize his position thus:

> Thus it appears reasonable to suppose that it was what God had respect to as an ultimate end of his creating the world, to communicate of his own infinite fullness of good; or rather it was his last end, that there might be a glorious and abundant emanation of his infinite fullness of good *ad extra,* or without himself, and the disposition to communicate himself or diffuse his own *fullness,* which we must conceive of as being originally in God as a perfection of his nature, was what moved him to create the world . . . Therefore, to speak more strictly according to truth,

115. Edwards, *Ethical Writings*, 432–33.

> we may suppose, *that a disposition in God, as an original property of his nature, to an emanation of his own infinite fullness, was what excited him to create the world; and so that the emanation itself was aimed at by him as a last end of the creation.*[116]

Perhaps the most striking feature of these paragraphs is Edwards's reiterated use of the word "emanation": "emanation *ad extra*"; "such an emanation of good"; "the emanation, which is as it were an increase, repetition, or multiplication of it"; "so these should have an emanation"; "a glorious and abundant emanation of his infinite fulness of good *ad extra,* or without himself"; "an emanation of his own infinite fulness." It should be noted that Edwards makes considerable use of the word "emanation" elsewhere in the dissertation. Throughout the dissertation, the creation is viewed as an emanation of God's fullness, an emanation of God's glory, an emanation *ad extra.* "What is striking in this argument," observes Anri Morimoto, "is the fact that he did not hesitate to use emanationist language at all."[117]

In the light of this reiterated use of the word "emanation," the question that obviously arises is this: Is Edwards espousing here some form of emanationism? Is he endorsing the tradition of Christian Neoplatonism? If so, is he a panentheist? According to the traditional emanation theory of creation, the world is regarded as a necessary efflux or emanation out of the divine being. Creation is viewed as emanating at every successive moment out of the mysterious Absolute or One. Yet God and the universe are viewed as basically one, the universe being the phenomenal manifestation of God. It should be noted, moreover, that in this dissertation, Edwards also utilizes the classic Neoplatonic images of "the fountain that overflows" and of "the sun that constantly shines" in order to describe the creative activity of God. Edwards represents God as diffusing himself, as communicating himself, as enlarging himself, as shining forth and overflowing, in short, as emanating himself in the creation. God has an essential disposition to create, and the creation itself is construed, daringly, as "an increase, repetition, or multiplication" of the Creator. Moreover, there is within the dissertation itself an internal consistency about these Neoplatonic strands. Conversely, indeed significantly, one looks in vain in this dissertation for an emphasis upon divine fiat or *creatio ex nihilo;* the emphasis falls, rather, upon the dynamic self-movement of God.

In his recent study of panentheism, John W. Cooper utilizes the definition of panentheism provided by *The Oxford Dictionary of the Christian Church:* "The Being of God includes and penetrates the whole universe,

116. Edwards, *Ethical Writings*, 433–35.

117. Morimoto, "End for Which," 42.

so that every part exists in Him, but His Being is more than, and not exhausted by, the universe."[118] "In other words," Cooper comments, "God and the world are ontologically distinct and God transcends the world, but the world is in God ontologically."[119] "Panentheism is the view that all things exist within the being of God but that God's being nevertheless transcends them."[120] Cooper is careful to sound certain caveats with regard to the putative co-extensiveness of Neoplatonism and panentheism, but concedes that "it is accurate to say that the history of panentheism is largely the history of Neoplatonism."[121] "Neoplatonism," he insists, "is the genuine fountainhead of classical panentheism."[122] "Neoplatonism is panentheistic because everything exists within God in a series of concentric emanations . . . Much panentheism carries on the transcendent-immanent theology of Neoplatonism."[123] In view of Edwards's use of both the language and the central concepts of Neoplatonism in *God's Chief End*, the question that inevitably arises is this: Is Edwards's position in this treatise that of panentheism?

Crisp contends, strongly, that Edwards's Neoplatonism necessarily entails panentheism: "First, it would appear that Neoplatonism does indeed yield panentheism. And, second, it does appear that Edwards is both a Neoplatonist and panentheist."[124] Crisp defines panentheism thus: "God is to the world as the soul is to the body. The world is contained 'within' God, but God is not exhausted by the world; he is greater than the world."[125] It should be noted that this is precisely the analogy that Edwards uses in *God's Chief End* when he refers to the divine being, remarkably, as "the common soul of the universe."[126] Such language on Edwards's part (notably absent from

118. Cooper, *Panentheism*, 27.

119. Cooper, *Panentheism*, 27.

120. Cooper, *Panentheism*, 32.

121. Cooper, *Panentheism*, 19.

122. Cooper, *Panentheism*, 39.

123. Cooper, *Panentheism*, 18–19.

124. Crisp, "Jonathan Edwards's Panentheism," 120.

125. Crisp, *Among the Theologians*, 173.

126. Edwards, *Ethical Writings*, 425. "He would therefore determine that the whole universe, including all creatures animate and inanimate, in all its actings, proceedings, revolutions, and entire series of events, should proceed from a regard and with a view to God, as the supreme and last end of all: that every wheel, both great and small, in all its rotations, should move with a constant invariable regard to him as the ultimate end of all; as perfectly and uniformly as if the whole system were animated and directed by one common soul: or, as if such an arbiter as I have before supposed, one possessed of perfect wisdom and rectitude, became the common soul of the universe, and actuated and governed it in all its motions." Edwards, *Ethical Writings*, 424–25. Elwood comments thus: "This Neoplatonic idea of 'one common soul' animating and directing

his sermons, but present in his philosophical writings) appears to align itself with the concept of "the World-Soul" found in Neoplatonism. Cooper concludes, significantly, that "Edwards lacks the robust ontological Creator-creature distinction of classical theism."[127] "Edwards's philosophy of nature hovers between pantheism and panentheism."[128]

Moreover, Crisp views Edwards's panentheism within the larger context of the latter's idealism and occasionalism:

> Rather, he comes to his panentheism through careful reflection on the doctrine of God as well as on the basis of philosophical assumptions, such as his idealism and his occasionalism. Or, to put it another way, Edwards was "grasping for a third alternative" between classical theism and pantheism, that "would do justice on the one hand to God's all-comprehensiveness, and on the other, to His creative presence in the world."[129]

Indeed, Crisp describes Edwards as "an idealist panentheist"[130]—for Edwards, the world is "a series of ideal momentary world-stages in the divine mind":[131]

> But this means that all created entities are mind-dependent in a radical way. We all exist provided God continues to think us because all created existence is ideal. In which case, Edwards's position entails antirealism, where antirealism is the view according to which there is no mind-independent reality . . . Not only is it the case on an Edwardsian ontology that the created order is the ideal, necessary product of an essentially creative deity; it is also the case that the created order has no existence independent of God; it does not—indeed, cannot—perdure. God creates the world at one moment, but the world immediately ceases to exist, and is replaced by a numerically distinct world-stage that is qualitatively near identical to the previous world-stage (the relevant incremental changes having been

---

the universe is an unusual expression, even for Edwards. . . We have already seen how Edwards felt that Calvin, in rejecting pantheism, had also rejected the Christian element of truth in pantheism, which Augustine had exploited." Elwood, *Philosophical Theology*, 176–77.

127. Cooper, *Panentheism*, 77.

128. Cooper, *Panentheism*, 75.

129. Crisp, *Edwards as Contemporary*, 107–8.

130. Crisp, *Edwards as Contemporary*, 122.

131. Crisp, *Edwards as Contemporary*, 115.

> built-in to the second world stage to give the appearance of change across time).[132]

Thus Crisp views Edwards's doctrine of continuous creation in an essentially idealist, immaterialist, antirealist context. The world exists truly and only in the mind of God; there is no mind-independent reality—there is no God-independent reality. The world exists only insofar as God continues to "think the world." Thus in Edwards's system God not only continuously *thinks of the world;* he also continuously *thinks the world;* that is to say, he continuously *thinks the world into existence.* This is the radical mind-dependence that characterizes the creation in Edwards's thought and this is the intriguing twist that Edwards imparts to his idealism: the creation is construed as radically dependent upon the thinking of God. If God were to cease "thinking the world," the world itself would necessarily cease to exist. Thus God's continuous "thinking the world" correlates to God's continuous creation of the world. We note here the logical connection, indeed, the intrinsic coherence, between Edwards's idealism, his antirealism, his doctrine of continuous creation, his concept of temporal parts, the moment-by-moment dependence of the cosmos upon God, his ambivalence with regard to the concept of mechanism, his suppression of the concept of second causes, his extraordinary emphasis upon divine immediacy, and his occasionalism. "For on an Edwardsian way of thinking," Crisp contends, "the creation is a radically contingent, momentary set of ideas that are world-stages generated seriatim according to divine convention in God's mind. God and his self-communication in creation are distinct all right. But the world only exists in God."[133]

ISAAC NEWTON AND THE APPLE

Let us note, in conclusion, the implications and the ramifications of Edwards's position with regard to God and the creation in the context of an alleged scene from history; namely, the legendary tale of Sir Isaac Newton and the falling apple: Edwards's Neoplatonic panentheism requires that we view Isaac Newton and the falling apple as part of that communication, that diffusion, that emanation of God's infinite fullness *ad extra* (towards the outside) that constitutes the creation of the cosmos; they are, quite simply, an infinitesimal part—minute droplets, in effect—of the "abundant

132. Crisp, *Edwards as Contemporary*, 114.

133. Crisp, *Edwards as Contemporary*, 119.

streams"[134] sent forth by the living God in creation. Sir Isaac and the apple, not to mention the apple tree, the garden, and the house adjoining, are all "in God"—they are somehow "contained in God." Does this mean, then, that Sir Isaac Newton is divine? Does it mean that the apple is divine? It is difficult to evade the conclusion that they are, in fact, in some sense divine. Morimoto notes "the ontological continuity between God and the world that the doctrine of emanation entails."[135] "Since both God and the world belong to the same hierarchical order, it degrades God to creatureliness while elevating the creature to divinity at the same time."[136] Edwards's emanationist panentheist position would appear to flirt and toy with the divinity of Sir Isaac Newton, the divinity of the apple, the divinity (in some sense) of the entire creation.

The paradox here is that there is a radical contingence, a moment-by-moment dependence on the part of the aforementioned—the paradox is, in short, that of the radical contingence of the quasi-divine. Edwards's doctrine of *creatio continua* requires that we view Sir Isaac Newton himself and the apple in terms of a doctrine of temporal parts—that we view them as re-created *de novo ex nihilo* (anew out of nothing) at every successive moment of this particular scene. It is clear that neither Newton nor the apple can perdure—indeed, the apple cannot even perdure in its fleeting journey to the ground. It is only because *God thinks the apple*—that is to say, it is only because *God continues to think the apple into existence*—that the apple actually reaches the ground. The body, the solidity, the motion, the very existence of the apple, not to mention the force of gravity itself, are all dependent upon the immediate power of God. The antecedent existence of both Newton and the apple does not account for their continuing existence, nor can their continued existence be explained simply as a matter of God's preservation. Their continued existence and even their respective movements are the direct result of the immediate activity of the Creator, who occasionalistically "conserves" both Newton and the apple, commensurate with the appearance of there being physical laws that persist through time. Thus, although there is the impression of permanence in this historic scene, it is only by the sovereign constitution of God that their identity through time is preserved. The changes in the position of the falling apple are marvelously built into God's continuous re-creation of the apple. Indeed, its apparent preservation is, quite simply, an illusion—a most amazing example, in fact, of *Sein und*

134. Edwards, *Ethical Writings*, 433.

135. Morimoto, "End for Which," 39.

136. Crisp, *Edwards as Contemporary*, 39.

Schein.[137] The *Schein* in this instance is that of a perfectly stable, numerically identical apple falling rapidly to the ground; the *Sein* in this instance is that of an astonishing series of numerically different facsimile apples, each of which is created *de novo ex nihilo* at every successive moment by God. Thus as the apple falls to the ground, so the multiple incremental differences in the position of the apple as a result of gravity, motion, and succession are incorporated into the general picture of the scene as it unfolds on "the silver screen of the divine mind." Moreover, while the force of gravity, which is responsible for the fall of the apple, can be explained in terms of mechanism and in terms of "natural necessity"[138]—more specifically, in terms of solidity and of matter acting upon matter—the force of gravity, in the final analysis, "depends immediately on the divine influence." In the final analysis, the law of gravity itself, which Sir Isaac Newton himself formulated, and that (so legend has it) largely as a result of this very scene, is, as Edwards himself puts it, but "the stated condition"—it is but "the stated method" of God's universal, omnipotent, and astonishingly immediate activity.

137. "Sein und Schein" is a term used in German literary criticism to denote the paradox of "appearance and reality." "Sein" corresponds to "reality" and "Schein" corresponds to "appearance."

138. Edwards, *Freedom of the Will*, 156. "By 'natural necessity,' as applied to men, I mean such necessity as men are under through the force of natural causes; as distinguished from what are called moral causes . . . so by a natural necessity men's bodies move downwards, when there is nothing to support them." Edwards, *Freedom of the Will*, 156–57.

THE WILL

FREEDOM OF THE WILL (1754)

It is a curious fact that, at first glance, Edwards's magisterial treatise, *Freedom of the Will*, does not appear to be particularly concerned with the concept of divine immediacy. The author of the treatise lives self-consciously in a distinctly heliocentric, post-Copernican, Newtonian cosmos that is subject to the reign of natural law. His passing references in the treatise to "the planet Jupiter,"[1] to "the revolution of a planet round the sun,"[2] to "the doctrine of the infinite divisibility of matter,"[3] to "established laws of nature,"[4] and his specific reference to Sir Isaac Newton all demonstrate incontrovertibly the pivotal fact of his acquaintance with and his acceptance of "the new astronomy" and "the new science" that had gripped the European mind increasingly on the publication of Newton's *Principia* in 1687:

> If the laws of motion, and gravitation, laid down by Sir Isaac Newton, hold universally, there is not one atom, nor the least assignable part of an atom, but what has influence, every moment, throughout the whole material universe, to cause every part to be otherwise than it would be, if it were not for that particular corporeal existence.[5]

1. Edwards, *Freedom of the Will*, 392.
2. Edwards, *Freedom of the Will*, 393.
3. Edwards, *Freedom of the Will*, 387.
4. Edwards, *Freedom of the Will*, 366.
5. Edwards, *Freedom of the Will*, 392–93.

It is an interesting fact that, in contrast to the youthful writings of the Yale student in the 1720s, the force of gravity is not ascribed here to the immediacy of God; it is ascribed to mechanism and natural law. Indeed, remarkably, there are, in this treatise, no references whatsoever to the immediate exercise of divine power in the created order.

Moreover, in contrast to *Original Sin* (1758), there is in *Freedom of the Will* no reference at all to continuous creation. The tacit assumption throughout the treatise is that of a single act of creation in the beginning. Indeed, the tacit assumption is, as in the Scriptures, that of two distinct phases of activity; namely, an initial act of creation and an ongoing preservation. God is described as "the maker, owner, and supreme governor of the world"[6]—the God who created in the past and who preserves in the present—not, ostensibly, the God who re-creates all things *ex nihilo* at every successive moment. The treatise appears to make a distinction between the unique act of creation in the beginning and the constant, ongoing act of preservation since.

Indeed, it is a striking fact that Edwards's world in *Freedom of the Will* is portrayed as a fixed, settled, stable, orderly, established world governed by natural law. Edwards refers throughout the treatise to "established laws of nature"[7] and "the established course of things."[8] Edwards's world in this treatise is a world characterized by mechanism, by cause and effect, by antecedents and consequents, and by the necessary connection between them. His main focus in the essay is, of course, clearly upon the mental, moral world; but there are also numerous references and allusions to the physical, material world. Certainly, Edwards makes it abundantly clear that both this world and these laws are subject to "the sovereign Creator and Disposer of the world,"[9] and that he may choose, sovereignly, to intervene and interpose supernaturally, indeed immediately, at times. Nevertheless, such interventions and interpositions are represented as the exception, not the rule; the rule is clearly that of the reign of natural law under the dominion of the Creator. Edwards constantly gives the impression in this treatise that he views the cosmos as governed, not so much immediately, as mediately, via mechanism—the mechanism that he, paradoxically, both asserted and denied in his youth. It is interesting to note that in *Freedom of the Will*, he asserts mechanism without also denying it. In fact, a good case can be made that here, in his most famous work, Edwards, at first glance, emerges much

6. Edwards, *Freedom of the Will*, 411.
7. Edwards, *Freedom of the Will*, 366.
8. Edwards, *Freedom of the Will*, 367.
9. Edwards, *Freedom of the Will*, 432.

more as the champion of the concept of mediacy than as the champion of the concept of immediacy.

Thus the concept of divine immediacy appears, in his *magnum opus,* to be conspicuous by its absence. *Freedom of the Will* does not, therefore, appear to contribute very much to the thesis that this particular concept constitutes the controlling idea and the correlating principle in his *oeuvre;* indeed, at first glance, Edwards's celebrated essay appears, to some extent, to be an embarrassment to this thesis. The word "immediate," so prominent in Edwards's writings as a whole, occurs relatively rarely, and the concept of immediacy appears to be surprisingly suppressed. Certainly, there is, as the essay develops, an increasing emphasis upon the First Cause, "the all-wise determiner of all events."[10] But even this emphasis upon the First Cause does not go hand in hand with a strong emphasis upon divine immediacy. Second causes, mechanism, the concept of natural law, cause and effect, determinism—these are the concepts that clearly lie to the fore.

THE INFLUENCE OF MOTIVES

Edwards's analysis of the influence of motives upon the will must be viewed in this context of the universal concatenation of cause and effect. "To talk of the determination of the will, supposes an effect, which must have a cause. If the will be determined, there is a determiner,"[11] insists Edwards at the very outset of his essay. What, then, or who, is the "determiner" of the will? Is it motives? Is it the self? Or is it God? Or is it a combination of some or all of these? Edwards soon answers that question, at least in part: "It is that motive, which, as it stands in the view of the mind, is the strongest, that determines the will."[12] More precisely, Edwards defines the will as determined by "the strongest motive,"[13] "the greatest apparent good,"[14] and "the last dictate of the understanding."[15] His reasoning here is, quite simply, that motives are causes—causes that produce effects. Edwards is concerned to establish the concatenation of all events. "I assert," he insists, "that nothing ever comes to pass without a cause."[16]

10. Edwards, *Freedom of the Will*, 410.
11. Edwards, *Freedom of the Will*, 141.
12. Edwards, *Freedom of the Will*, 141.
13. Edwards, *Freedom of the Will*, 142.
14. Edwards, *Freedom of the Will*, 143.
15. Edwards, *Freedom of the Will*, 148.
16. Edwards, *Freedom of the Will*, 185.

> So that it is indeed as repugnant to reason, to suppose that an act of the will should come into existence without a cause, as to suppose the human soul, or an angel, or the globe of the earth, or the whole universe, should come into existence without a cause.[17]

> Every act of the will has a cause, or it has not. If it has a cause, then, according to what has already been demonstrated, it is not contingent, but necessary; the effect being necessarily dependent and consequent on its cause; and that, let the cause be what it will.[18]

Thus motives exert "causal influence"; they constitute "a ground of existence by positive influence."[19] Motives thus constitute the "determiner" of the will. Edwards emerges at this point in the essay as the proponent of a powerful determinism. Moreover, it is important to note that, for much of the essay, this determinism operates on the horizontal level. Edwards's whole argument rests upon what he terms the "connection of causes and effects."[20] This general, indeed universal, concatenation of all events is appropriately illustrated by his reiterated use of the metaphor of "the chain."[21] It should be noted that Edwards has in mind here not only the endless chain of events in the physical, natural world, but also that which obtains in the mental, moral world—the world of motives, choices, and actions on the part of humanity—and the complex interaction of these two worlds. In the early part of the essay especially, Edwards emerges basically as a horizontal determinist.

It will be immediately evident that Edwards's concept of the motivation and the operation of the will necessarily presupposes a process—a process which, by definition, involves the passage of time:

> And I think it must also be allowed by all, that everything that is properly called a motive, excitement or inducement to a perceiving, willing agent, has some sort and degree of tendency, or advantage to move or excite the will, previous to the effect, or to the act of the will excited. This previous tendency of the motive is what I call the "strength" of the motive. That motive which has a less degree of previous advantage or tendency to move the will, or that appears less inviting, as it stands in the view of the mind, is what I call a "weaker motive." On the contrary, that which

17. Edwards, *Freedom of the Will*, 185.
18. Edwards, *Freedom of the Will*, 270.
19. Edwards, *Freedom of the Will*, 237.
20. Edwards, *Freedom of the Will*, 180.
21. See Edwards, *Freedom of the Will*, 367.

> appears most inviting, and has, by what appears concerning it to the understanding or apprehension, the greatest degree of previous tendency to excite and induce the choice, is what I call the "strongest motive." And in this sense, I suppose the will is always determined by the strongest motive.[22]

Indeed, Edwards's own definition here not only presupposes the passage of time, but also specifically alludes to the passage of time with his reiterated use of the word "previous": "previous to the effect"; "this previous tendency of the motive"; "a less degree of previous advantage"; "the greatest degree of previous tendency"; "motives, exhibiting and operating previous to the act of the will."[23] Moreover, Edwards's use of phrases such as "antecedent bias,"[24] "prior inclination,"[25] "all antecedent preponderation or inclination,"[26] "antecedent preponderation of the will"[27] again demonstrates that, in dealing with the psychological processes of humanity, he is thinking in temporal terms. His terminology proves incontrovertibly that which, in the very nature of things, is self-evident; namely, that the cause is temporally prior to the effect. Inevitably involved and constantly assumed, in his concept of the process of the motivation of the will, is the passage of time.

THE TENSION IN EDWARDS'S THOUGHT

It is at this point that we note a *prima facie* tension in Edwards's thought—indeed, what is, potentially, a major philosophical and theological inconsistency—namely, the apparent tension between the horizontal and the vertical dimension in his system. More precisely, there appears, at first glance, to be a real tension between the determinism of *Freedom of the Will* and the continuous creation doctrine of *Original Sin*. In the former treatise, Edwards insists upon the temporal causation of events; in the latter, he insists upon a doctrine of temporal parts. In the former treatise, Edwards insists upon the effect of "antecedent bias";[28] in the latter, he denies the effect of "antecedent existence."[29] According to Edwards, "antecedent existence" does not account

22. Edwards, *Freedom of the Will*, 142.
23. Edwards, *Freedom of the Will*, 424.
24. Edwards, *Freedom of the Will*, 205.
25. Edwards, *Freedom of the Will*, 205.
26. Edwards, *Freedom of the Will*, 204.
27. Edwards, *Freedom of the Will*, 205.
28. Edwards, *Freedom of the Will*, 205.
29. Edwards, *Original Sin*, 400.

for subsequent existence; yet "antecedent bias" supposedly accounts for subsequent choice. For Edwards, there is clearly no independent continuity inherent in created existence; yet determinism clearly presupposes such a continuity. The problem is, quite simply, that the concatenation of events predicated in the essay of 1754 is, according to the essay of 1758, continuously interrupted *de novo* at every successive moment by God's continuous creation of all things *ex nihilo.* It will be immediately obvious not only that continuous creation on the one hand and determinism on the other appear to be strange bedfellows in Edwards's system, but also that, as such, they appear to be mutually destructive. "Now," it is tempting to ask in Edwardsian fashion, "how can these things hang together?"[30]

VERTICAL DETERMINISM

It is important to note at this point, however, that the horizontal line of the temporal causation of events turns sharply upwards in the latter part of Edwards's treatise—indeed, that this horizontal determinism gives way to a powerful vertical determinism. Edwards makes it abundantly clear, as he moves towards the climax of his argument, that his doctrine of the temporal causation of events must be viewed *sub specie aeternitatis* (from the vantage point of eternity). It is at this point that Edwards's doctrine of necessity merges with what he describes as "the absolute, and most perfect sovereignty of God";[31] indeed, Edwards even speaks of "the Calvinistic doctrine of necessity."[32] This doctrine of the intrinsic inevitability of all things is strengthened, in Edwards's view, firstly, by the fact of God's promise of certain things: "God's absolute promise of any things makes the things promised *necessary,* and their failing to take place absolutely *impossible*";[33] and secondly, by the fact of God's prescience of all things: "If, strictly speaking, there is no foreknowledge in God, 'tis because those things which are future to us, are as present to God, as if they already had existence: and that is as much as to say, that future events are always in God's view as evident, clear, sure, and necessary, as if they already were."[34] It is, in the final analysis, the immediacy of God's knowledge that makes the concept of God's prescience, strictly speaking, redundant.

30. See Edwards, *Freedom of the Will,* 227.
31. Edwards, *Freedom of the Will,* 378.
32. Edwards, *Freedom of the Will,* 420.
33. Edwards, *Freedom of the Will,* 283.
34. Edwards, *Freedom of the Will,* 267.

Indeed, Edwards specifically emphasizes the following with regard to "men's volitions, and all moral events":[35] "Therefore the sovereignty of God doubtless extends to this matter."[36] Thus, while on the horizontal dimension Edwards views humanity's volitions as determined by "the strongest motive," "the greatest apparent good," and "the last dictate of the understanding," on the vertical dimension he views God as the ultimate determiner of their volitions. Edwards's descriptions of God are of great significance at this point—he specifically describes God as "the supreme and absolute Governor of the universe,"[37] "the all-wise determiner of all events,"[38] and "the supreme orderer of all things":[39]

> It properly belongs to the supreme and absolute Governor of the universe, to order all important events within his dominion, by his wisdom: but the events in the moral world are of the most important kind; such as the moral actions of intelligent creatures, and their consequences.
>
> These events will be ordered by something. They will either be disposed by wisdom, or they will be disposed by chance; that is, they will be disposed by blind and undesigning causes, if that were possible, and could be called a disposal. Is it not better, that the good and evil which happens in God's world, should be ordered, regulated, bounded and determined by the good pleasure of an infinitely wise Being, who perfectly comprehends within his understanding and constant view, the universality of things, in all their extent and duration, and sees all the influence of every event, with respect to every individual thing and circumstance, throughout the grand system, and the whole of the eternal series of consequences; than to leave these things to fall out by chance, and to be determined by those causes which have no understanding or aim?[40]

Thus in the closing stages of the essay, Edwards makes abundantly clear his fundamental, overarching commitment to "the doctrine of an universal determining providence."[41] It is important to note that, at this point, Edwards emerges increasingly as a vertical determinist—the horizontal dimension is,

35. Edwards, *Freedom of the Will*, 405.
36. Edwards, *Freedom of the Will*, 405.
37. Edwards, *Freedom of the Will*, 404.
38. Edwards, *Freedom of the Will*, 410.
39. Edwards, *Freedom of the Will*, 411.
40. Edwards, *Freedom of the Will*, 404–5.
41. Edwards, *Freedom of the Will*, 431.

in the final analysis, subordinate to the vertical dimension, and horizontal necessity subordinate to vertical necessity:

> Hereby it becomes manifest, that God's moral government over mankind, his treating them as moral agents, making them the objects of his commands, counsels, calls, warnings, expostulations, promises, threatenings, rewards and punishments, is not inconsistent with a determining disposal of all events, of every kind, throughout the universe, in his providence; either by positive efficiency, or permission. Indeed such an *universal, determining providence,* infers some kind of necessity of all events; such a necessity as implies an infallible previous fixedness of the futurity of the event: but no other necessity of moral events, or volitions of intelligent agents, is needful in order to this, than *moral* necessity; which does as much ascertain the futurity of the event as any other necessity . . . Yea, not only are objections of this kind against the doctrine of an universal determining providence, removed by what has been said; but the truth of such a doctrine is demonstrated. As it has been demonstrated, that the futurity of all future events is established by previous necessity, either natural or moral; so 'tis manifest, that the sovereign Creator and Disposer of the world has ordered this necessity, by ordering his own conduct, either in designedly acting, or forbearing to act. For, as the being of the world is from God, so the circumstances in which it had its being at first, both negative and positive, must be ordered by him, in one of these ways; and all the necessary consequences of these circumstances, must be ordered by him. And God's active and positive interpositions, after the world was created, and the consequences of these interpositions; also every instance of his forbearing to interpose, and the sure consequences of this forbearance, must all be determined according to his pleasure. And therefore every event which is the consequence of anything whatsoever, or that is connected with any foregoing thing or circumstance, either positive or negative, as the ground or reason of its existence, must be ordered of God; either by a designed efficiency and interposition, or a designed forbearing to operate or interpose. But, as has been proved, all events whatsoever are necessarily connected with something foregoing, either positive or negative, which is the ground of its existence. It follows, therefore, that the whole series of events is thus connected with something in the state of things either positive or negative, which is original in the series; i.e. something which is connected with nothing preceding that, but God's own immediate conduct, either his acting or

> forbearing to act. From whence it follows, that as God designedly orders his own conduct, and its connected consequences, it must necessarily be, that he designedly orders all things.[42]

It should be noted here that, in his analysis of the concatenation of all events, Edwards traces the connection between cause and effect, between antecedents and consequents, horizontally back along the infinite series or chain of events, and comes, in the final analysis, to that which is "original in the series"; namely, "God's own immediate conduct, either his acting or forbearing to act."[43] This is, remarkably, one of the very few occasions when Edwards utilizes the word "immediate" in *Freedom of the Will.* He traces here the endless links in the chain back to the First Cause, so that, in the final analysis, all the intervening mediateness of secondary causes is traced back to the immediacy of the First Cause, "the sovereign Creator and Disposer of the world."[44] Edwards acknowledges here that God is the ultimate, although not the proximate, cause of all things. He thus postulates here a kind of deferred, ultimate immediacy on the part of God—an immediacy that coheres with his vertical determinism. It should be noted, however, that there is nothing radical about this species of divine immediacy. Thus, in the final analysis, it is not motives, but God, who is the determiner of the will; all people everywhere, all things everywhere, all events, all circumstances, at all times, Edwards insists, are in the hands of God, "the sovereign Lord of the universe."[45] "Edwards," Crisp insists, "was a *global* theological determinist."[46]

THE CASE OF JUDAS

It is important to note that Edwards clearly sees no contradiction between the horizontal determinism involved in his concept of the temporal causation of all events and the vertical determinism involved in his concept of "an universal, determining providence";[47] he sees no contradiction between humanity's responsibility and God's sovereignty. Edwards's essentially compatibilist position with regard to this horizontal determinism on the one hand and this vertical determinism on the other hand is well illustrated by

42. Edwards, *Freedom of the Will*, 431–32.
43. Edwards, *Freedom of the Will*, 432.
44. Edwards, *Freedom of the Will*, 432.
45. Edwards, *Freedom of the Will*, 374.
46. Crisp, *God and Creation*, 65.
47. Edwards, *Freedom of the Will*, 431.

what Edwards refers to as "that great sin of Judas."[48] We note the fact that, on the horizontal level, Judas was one of the twelve apostles, that he had heard the call of the Son of Man to follow him, that he had accompanied Christ for some three years, that he had even preached the Word of God to others, that he had, presumably, performed miracles in Christ's name, and that he had constantly heard from the lips of his Master those spiritual motives which emphasized the importance of seeking first the kingdom of God and his righteousness. But Judas "had the bag" (John 12:6) and, as such, he was tempted to covetousness. Thus it is evident that, in the course of time, there arose a conflicting set of motives in Judas's heart and mind. On the one hand, there lay before him the motive of following and serving Christ with the reward of treasure in heaven; on the other hand, there lay before him the motive of betraying Christ with the reward of treasure on earth. In the final analysis, the prospect of obtaining thirty pieces of silver proved to be "the strongest motive" and "the greatest apparent good"; this wicked, powerful desire was "the last dictate of the understanding." In all of this, Judas acted as a free, voluntary agent, he acted according to his desires (this is "the liberty of spontaneity")[49] and he was responsible for his own treachery. The desire for thirty pieces of silver was the cause; the betrayal of the Messiah with a kiss was the effect.

Conversely, on the vertical dimension we note that, as Edwards puts it, "the treachery of Judas . . . was ordered in God's providence, in pursuance of his purpose."[50] This vertical determinism expresses the purpose and the sovereignty of God in this matter. The first of Edwards's several references to Judas in *Freedom of the Will* occurs in the context of "God's certain foreknowledge of the volitions of moral agents."[51] His basic thesis here is this: "That the acts of the wills of moral agents are not contingent events, in that sense, as to be without all necessity, appears by God's certain foreknowledge of such events."[52] Edwards's argument here is, quite simply, that the divine foreknowledge of an event entails the necessity or the ultimate inevitability of the event. Thus, if God foretells an event, then God foreknows that event, and if God foreknows the event, then the event itself is utterly certain and absolutely inevitable. Thus Judas's act of betraying Christ was not a contingent event; God's prescience or certain foreknowledge of this act of betrayal, as evidenced by God's specific prediction of this event, necessarily entailed

48. Edwards, *Freedom of the Will*, 241.
49. See Crisp, *God and Creation*, 70.
50. Edwards, *Freedom of the Will*, 402.
51. Edwards, *Freedom of the Will*, 239.
52. Edwards, *Freedom of the Will*, 239.

what Edwards describes as "an infallible previous fixedness of the futurity of the event."[53]

But if there is, in the final analysis, no contradiction or incompatibility between Edwards's horizontal determinism and his vertical determinism, there is, potentially, a very significant contradiction and incompatibility between his horizontal determinism and his vertical occasionalism. This is the *prima facie* tension in Edwards's thought. On the horizontal dimension, Edwards (by clear implication) views Judas as responding, in the course of time, to the ever strengthening motive of the prospect of filthy lucre; but on the vertical dimension, Edwards is clearly committed to the view that, at every successive moment, Judas is re-created by God *ex nihilo.* Not only is the vertical dimension at odds here with the horizontal dimension; the vertical dimension is continually cutting across the horizontal dimension and effectively undermining its reality. Thus on the horizontal dimension, we are left with (as Malebranche puts it) "causes that are not causes at all." The necessary connection between the cause in this case (the motive of thirty pieces of silver) and the effect (the actual act of betrayal of Christ with a kiss) is, according to Edwards's doctrine of continuous creation, interrupted *de novo* at every successive moment by God's re-creation of the traitor. If we are to take Edwards seriously with regard to continuous creation, there is, strictly speaking, no mundane causation; there are, strictly speaking, no series of causes-and-effects, but only effects—in fact, an infinite series of new effects, each one of which is produced immediately by the First Cause himself. If God re-creates Judas at every successive moment *ex nihilo,* then it is surely impossible to avoid the conclusion that God re-creates Judas at the very moment of betrayal—indeed, that he effectively creates the act of betrayal itself.

IS EDWARDS'S GOD THE AUTHOR OF SIN?

The question that inevitably arises at this point is this: Is it not the case that Edwards's doctrine of continuous creation and its inevitable corollary—some form of occasionalism—necessarily mean that God is the author of sin, indeed, that God is, in effect, the actor of sin? This particular charge is, of course, a charge that is consistently leveled by Arminians against non-occasionalist Calvinists on account of their Calvinism, and Edwards responds to *that* charge towards the close of his essay, in the section entitled, "Concerning that objection against the doctrine which has been maintained, that it makes God the Author of Sin":

53. Edwards, *Freedom of the Will*, 431.

> 'Tis urged by Arminians, that the doctrine of the necessity of men's volitions, or their necessary connection with antecedent events and circumstances, makes the First Cause, and supreme orderer of all things, the author of sin; in that he has so constituted the state and course of things, that sinful volitions become necessary, in consequence of his disposal.[54]

Edwards concedes that God is "the permitter, or not a hinderer of sin."[55] Indeed, he insists that God permits sin (i.e., he does not hinder it) "for wise, holy, and most excellent ends and purposes." Edwards illustrates this important principle by means of a reference to "the whole affair of Christ's crucifixion"[56]:

> 'Tis certain, that God thus, for excellent, holy, gracious and glorious ends, ordered the fact which they committed, who were concerned in Christ's death; and that therein they did but fulfil God's designs. As I trust, no Christian will deny it was the design of God, that Christ should be *crucified,* and that for this end he came into the world. 'Tis very manifest by many scriptures, that the whole affair of Christ's crucifixion, with its circumstances, and the treachery of Judas, that made way for it, was ordered in God's providence, in pursuance of his purpose.[57]

It is important to note Edwards's specific reference to Judas at this point. His argument here is that God permitted, and did not hinder, the treachery of Judas. Indeed, it was the design of God and ordered in God's providence:

> That there is a great difference between God's being concerned thus, by his *permission,* in an event and act, which in the inherent subject and agent of it, is sin (though the event will certainly follow on his permission), and his being concerned in it by *producing* it and exerting the act of sin; or between his being the *orderer* of its certain existence, by not *hindering* it, under certain circumstances, and his being the proper *actor* or *author* of it, by a *positive agency* or *efficiency.*[58]

It is at this point in his argument that Edwards introduces his pivotal analogy of the sun. He argues that, whereas the sun is the cause of light and heat, it is not the cause of darkness and cold; rather, it is the occasion of darkness

54. Edwards, *Freedom of the Will*, 397.
55. Edwards, *Freedom of the Will*, 399.
56. Edwards, *Freedom of the Will*, 402.
57. Edwards, *Freedom of the Will*, 402.
58. Edwards, *Freedom of the Will*, 403.

and cold. In this, Edwards contends, the sun is not *causa efficiens* (an efficent cause), but *causa deficiens* (a deficient cause):

> As there is a vast difference between the sun's being the cause of the lightsomeness and warmth of the atmosphere, and the brightness of gold and diamonds, by its presence and positive influence; and its being the occasion of darkness and frost, in the night, by its motion, whereby it descends below the horizon. The motion of the sun is the occasion of the latter kind of events; but it is not the proper cause, efficient, or producer of them; though they are necessarily consequent on that motion, under such circumstances: no more is any action of the divine Being the cause of the evil of men's wills. If the sun were the proper *cause* of cold and darkness, it would be the *fountain* of these things, as it is the fountain of light and heat: and then something might be argued from the nature of cold and darkness, to a likeness of nature in the sun; and it might be justly inferred, that the sun itself is dark and cold, and that his beams are black and frosty. But from its being the cause no otherwise than by its departure, no such thing can be inferred, but the contrary; it may justly be argued, that the sun is a bright and hot body, if cold and darkness are found to be the consequence of its withdrawment; and the more constantly and necessarily these effects are connected with, and confined to its absence, the more strongly does it argue the sun to be the fountain of light and heat. So, inasmuch as sin is not the fruit of any positive agency or influence of the most High, but on the contrary, arises from the withholding of his action and energy, and under certain circumstances, necessarily follows on the want of his influence; this is no argument that he is sinful, or his operation evil, or has anything of the nature of evil; but on the contrary, that he, and his agency, are altogether good and holy, and that he is the fountain of all holiness. It would be strange arguing indeed, because men never commit sin, but only when God leaves 'em *to themselves*, and necessarily sin, when he does so, that therefore their sin is not *from themselves*, but from God; and so, that God must be a sinful being: as strange as it would be to argue, because it is always dark when the sun is gone, and never dark when the sun is present, that therefore all darkness is from the sun, and that his disk and beams must needs be black.[59]

Thus, by means of this remarkable analogy, Edwards seeks to demonstrate that, just as the sun is "not the proper cause, efficient, or producer" of

59. Edwards, *Freedom of the Will*, 404.

darkness and cold, so God is not the author of sin—he is not the author of "the treachery of Judas." At first glance, it might appear that Edwards has produced here a brilliant and unanswerable analogy; but, as is often the case with analogical reasoning, there is a problem inherent in the analogy itself. Crisp offers the following critique of this analogy of the sun: "Unfortunately, this analogy will not yield the result that Edwards needs. For the sun, unlike God, is not a moral agent. If it were, then it *would* be the author of the resulting cold and dark, since it would be acting as a voluntary agent in bringing about the state of affairs where darkness obtains."[60] Edwards's analogy of the sun does not, in and of itself, exonerate Edwards's theology from the charge that it makes God the author of sin.

There is, however, an even greater residual problem for Edwards at this point—a problem that is inextricably related to his tremendous emphasis upon the immediacy of God as evidenced by his doctrine of continuous creation. If it is relatively easy to exonerate Edwards the Calvinist from the charge of making God the author of sin (albeit not via the analogy of the sun), it is surely much more difficult to exonerate Edwards the occasionalist from the same charge. Crisp expresses the problem created by Edwards's continuous creation-plus-occasionalism position thus:

> Matters are complicated by the fact that Edwards maintains more than a theological determinism . . . He was an occasionalist . . . But his occasionalism means that any distinction between permission and positive agency is undermined. For if there are no real causes apart from God's causal agency, then God's permission of x cannot mean anything less than his bringing x to pass, since any agent other than God has no ability to act as a cause whatsoever. But if it means this, then there is little or no difference between permission, on an occasionalistic view of God's causal action in the world, and positive agency. For God is the only causal agent.[61]

After all, Edwards's doctrine of continuous creation, when pressed to its logical conclusion, necessarily entails that God not only creates all things *ex nihilo* at every successive moment, but also that he created "the son of perdition" himself *ex nihilo* at every successive moment. Edwards the Calvinist can argue, with some cogency, that his Calvinistic system does not make God the author of Judas's treachery—God was only concerned in this "by his permission," not "by producing it"; but Edwards the occasionalist can, surely, scarcely argue that his occasionalistic system does not make God

60. Crisp, *Metaphysics of Sin*, 64.

61. Crisp, *Metaphysics of Sin*, 64.

the author of Judas's treachery, since, by clear implication, it specifically insists that Judas's continued existence cannot be explained by his antecedent existence—God was very much concerned in this matter, and that (to use Edwards's own language) "by a positive agency or efficiency";[62] namely, that of producing him! Edwards's extraordinary doctrine of continuous creation clearly exposes him to the charge of making God the author, indeed, the actor, not only of sin, but also of the sinner himself, and that at the very moment of his sin! On occasionalist principles, the putative *causa deficiens* is, surely, inevitably transmuted into *causa efficiens.*[63]

The issue, quite simply, then, is that Edwards's occasionalism appears to create very significant problems with regard to the internal consistency and coherence of his philosophical-theological system, and most notably of all with regard to his hamartiology. Crisp contends that "Edwards's theory of occasionalism is the single greatest flaw in his doctrine of sin."[64] If, as Edwards insists in *Original Sin,* all things are created *de novo ex nihilo* at every successive moment, then nothing persists through time, nothing can perdure, we have a doctrine of temporal parts, God is the sole causal agent in the universe, and there is no such thing as mundane or secondary causation. Edwards's occasionalism buttresses and bolsters, it seems, his doctrine of the absolute sovereignty of God; but it does so, surely, at the expense of the concept of human moral responsibility. God is the sole causal agent in the universe and God is also the sole moral agent in the universe, and since God is morally responsible for all creaturely actions, he is responsible for Adam's sin, he is responsible for Judas's sin, he is responsible for the sin of all people everywhere at all times. The irony here is that, as Crisp points out, "Edwards has undermined the very doctrine of sin he set out to defend."[65] "It is . . . a 'charming irony' that the very metaphysical notion Edwards deploys to defend his doctrine of imputation, ends up undercutting it."[66] Crisp

62. Edwards, *Freedom of the Will*, 403.

63. It is, interestingly, in the context of the thought of Jonathan Edwards himself that Charles Hodge makes this general observation with regard to the concept of continuous creation: "On this theory there can be no responsibility, no sin, and no holiness. If sin exist, it must be referred to God as much as holiness, for all is due to his creating energy." Hodge, *Systematic Theology*, 1.580. Hodge continues: "Between this system and Pantheism there is scarcely a dividing line. Pantheism merges the universe in God, but not more effectually than the doctrine of a continuous creation. God in the one case as truly as in the other, is all that lives. There is no power, no cause, no real existence but the efficiency and causality of God. This is obvious, and is generally admitted." Hodge, *Systematic Theology*, 1.580.

64. Crisp, *Metaphysics of Sin*, 130.

65. Crisp, *Metaphysics of Sin*, 132.

66. Crisp, *Metaphysics of Sin*, 132.

draws this conclusion with regard to Edwards's metaphysics: "[I]t appears that Edwards's God is the author of sin."[67]

A POSSIBLE RESOLUTION

Notwithstanding, then, the problems that Edwards's occasionalism obviously creates for his metaphysics of sin, the question that persists is this: Can the occasionalism of *Original Sin* be reconciled with the determinism of *Freedom of the Will?* In this context, it is important to note the cautious, guarded way in which Edwards, in *Freedom of the Will,* defines the term "cause":

> Therefore I sometimes use the word "cause," in this inquiry, to signify any antecedent, either natural or moral, positive or negative, on which an event, either a thing, or the manner and circumstance of a thing, so depends, that it is the ground and reason, either in whole, or in part, why it is, rather than not; or why it is as it is, rather than otherwise; or, in other words, any antecedent with which a consequent event is so connected, that it truly belongs to the reason why the proposition which affirms that event is true; whether it has any positive influence, or not. And in an agreeableness to this, I sometimes use the word "effect" for the consequence of another thing, which is perhaps rather an occasion than a cause, most properly speaking.[68]

What is so significant here is Edwards's careful use of synonyms for the word "cause." In this section he uses, in turn, the words "antecedent" ("any antecedent with which a consequent event is so connected"); "reason" ("some cause or reason"); "ground" ("the ground and reason"); and "occasion" ("which is perhaps rather an occasion than a cause"). Moreover, as he develops the concept of causality in the ensuing section, Edwards utilizes several times the phrase "a sufficient reason,"[69] as well as the phrase "a cause sufficient for the effect."[70] A little later, in the context of the non-contingency of volition, Edwards expresses his thought on causation thus: "And here it must be remembered . . . that nothing can ever come to pass without a cause, or reason why it exists in this manner rather than another; . . . inasmuch as those things which have a cause, or reason of their existence, must be

67. Crisp, *Metaphysics of Sin*, 133.

68. Edwards, *Freedom of the Will*, 180–81.

69. Edwards, *Freedom of the Will*, 186.

70. Edwards, *Freedom of the Will*, 186.

connected with their cause."[71] Moreover, towards the conclusion of the essay Edwards, in the course of summarizing his argument as a whole, emphasizes *inter alia* this fundamental principle: "[T]hat nothing can begin to be, which before was not, without a cause, or some antecedent ground or reason, why it then begins to be; that effects depend on their causes, and are connected with them."[72] The terminology and the concepts here appear to be Leibnizian: "There must be a sufficient reason," Leibniz insists, "(often known only to God), for anything to exist, for any event to occur, for any truth to obtain."[73] There is tantalizing evidence here that suggests that, in his concept of causation, Edwards embraces and utilizes Leibniz's principle of sufficient reason.[74]

What, then, is the significance of these Leibnizian overtones within Edwards's concept of causality in *Freedom of the Will?* Their significance lies in the fact that they leave the door open, in this treatise, for an occasionalist construction of God's relationship to the universe. It is important to note that Edwards's emphasis in the essay is not so much upon efficient causation, as upon connection or conjunction. In other words, it is not so much that, in Edwards's thought, the effect is efficiently produced by the cause; it is rather that the effect is connected with or conjoined to the cause. Edwards is, it appears, deliberately cautious and guarded with regard to "positive influence" and appears to shrink from asserting that what people generally denominate "the cause" produces what they denominate "the effect"; for Edwards such a *prima facie* cause is, rather, the "ground or reason" of the effect. Indeed, it is significant that Edwards actually employs the word "occasion" here. Thus, although Edwards does emerge at times as a horizontal determinist in *Freedom of the Will,* this determinism on his part should not be construed in hard, mechanistic, Newtonian terms. It is important to note that this crucial passage on causation, while not overtly or powerfully occasionalist in *malebranchiste* or even in classic Edwardsian fashion, is, in fact, compatible with an occasionalist construction of God's relationship to the universe. Certainly, the theological problem of God's being construed in this occasionalist construction as the author—indeed, as the actor—of sin remains; but the logical problem of the apparent incompatibility of the vertical and the horizontal dimension is resolved. Edwards's celebrated essay, for all of its relative silence with regard to the concept of divine immediacy,

71. Edwards, *Freedom of the Will*, 213.

72. Edwards, *Freedom of the Will*, 424.

73. Leibniz, *Philosophical Papers*, 613.

74. "Edwards espoused, probably without knowing it, Leibniz's principle of sufficient reason, namely, 'that nothing happens without a reason why it should be so, rather than otherwise.'" Fiering, *Edwards's Moral Thought*, 295.

does not, perhaps, in the final analysis, run counter to his colossal emphasis upon this theme throughout his *oeuvre* as a whole.

Another strand in the potential resolution of this issue is the possibility that, at this point in these two works, Edwards is dealing with matters at two different levels. It is quite possible that Edwards is making an implicit distinction here between, as Bishop George Berkeley (1685–1753) expresses it, "thinking with the learned" and "speaking with the vulgar"[75]—between, as Bishop Joseph Butler (1692–1752) expresses it, speaking in "a strict and philosophical sense" and speaking "in a loose and popular sense"?[76] By the time Edwards was publishing what Paul Ramsey has described as "his great, late works"[77] in the 1750s, both bishops were dead; but the distinction that they had made was clearly part of the philosophical spirit of the age. According to this view, Edwards can be construed as "thinking with the learned" and speaking in "a strict and philosophical sense" in his continuous creation-*cum*-occasionalism doctrine in *Original Sin,* and he can be construed as "speaking with the vulgar" and speaking in "a loose and popular sense" in his determinism in *Freedom of the Will*—in the former treatise he is utilizing the language of the philosopher and in the latter the language of the shop. Thus, according to this hypothesis, the seemingly irreconcilable problem is, in fact, fairly easily solved: the occasionalism of *Original Sin* emerges in the course of his metaphysical treatment of issues, while the determinism of *Freedom of the Will* emerges in the course of his non-theoretical treatment of issues. According to this hypothesis, Edwards's occasionalism obviously trumps his determinism; the vertical dimension, not surprisingly, trumps the horizontal dimension.

This line of interpretation would also explain why Edwards's continuous creation-plus-occasionalism doctrine is conspicuous by its absence in his sermons, whether in Northampton or in Stockbridge. Indeed, it is, surely, antecedently almost inconceivable that Edwards would have emphasized to the farmers and tradesmen of Northampton, still less to the Indians of Stockbridge, that the preacher who left the pulpit before their very eyes was not numerically the same as the preacher who entered the pulpit, or that they, his hearers, were not numerically identical with those who had taken their places in church approximately two hours earlier! Shrewdly, Edwards manifests in his pulpit utterances a certain reserve with regard to the more esoteric aspects of his concept of divine immediacy. He prefers, instead, to convey a sense of that immediacy via (for instance) the vivid, graphic image

75. Berkeley, *Treatise Concerning the Principles of Human Knowledge*, 222.

76. Butler, *Analogy of Religion*, 325.

77. Edwards, *Ethical Writings*, 9.

of the spider held over the fire—the sinner is, at all times and in all places, in the hands of God. In his sermons, Edwards was, not surprisingly, "speaking with the vulgar"—he was speaking in "a loose and popular sense." What is so interesting is that the immediacy of God implicit in the spider image is an expression, at a popular level, of Edwards's theoretical position. It is the sheer versatility of method with which Edwards conveys this enormous preoccupation with divine immediacy that is so striking.

THE SUPPRESSION OF THE CONCEPT OF MEANS

The sermon *A Divine and Supernatural Light*, however, appears to be an interesting exception to this general rule of reserve. The sermon was preached at Northampton in 1733 and, as Edwards himself observes in a footnote, it was "published at the desire of some of the hearers, in the year 1734."[78] It was one of Edwards's earliest publications. The significance of this rather sophisticated sermon lies in the fact that it provides an early, public treatment of the theme of divine immediacy in the realm of the will. Edwards's doctrine here is the following: "There is such a thing, as a spiritual and divine light, immediately imparted to the soul by God, of a different nature from any that is obtained by natural means."[79] The emphasis of the sermon falls unashamedly upon the immediacy of God in the regeneration of the sinner. In this sermon, Edwards establishes a very significant contrast between two different kinds of knowledge: that which "flesh and blood" reveals and that which "the Father" reveals. Edwards addresses the former species of knowledge first:

> God is the author of such knowledge; but yet not so but that flesh and blood reveals it. Mortal men are capable of imparting the knowledge of human arts and sciences, and skill in temporal affairs. God is the author of such knowledge by those means: flesh and blood is made use of by God as the mediate or second cause of it: he conveys it by the power and influence of natural means. But this spiritual knowledge, spoken of in the text, is what God is the author of, and none else: he reveals it, and flesh and blood reveals it not. He imparts this knowledge immediately, not making use of any intermediate natural causes, as he does in other knowledge.[80]

78. Hickman, *Works of Jonathan Edwards*, 2.12.
79. Edwards, *Sermons and Discourses, 1730–1733*, 410.
80. Edwards, *Sermons and Discourses, 1730–1733*, 409.

Thus "the knowledge of human arts and sciences" is a natural knowledge, imparted by second causes; it is a mediate knowledge. By contrast, "the spiritual knowledge spoken of in the text" is a supernatural knowledge, imparted by the First Cause; it is an immediate knowledge.

In the course of the sermon, Edwards makes this very significant statement in the context of the regeneration of the sinner: "God makes use of means; but 'tis not as mediate causes to produce this effect. There are not truly any second causes of it; but it is produced by God immediately. The Word of God is no proper cause of this effect."[81] The startling element here is, obviously, the denial that the Word of God is to be viewed as a mediate or second cause of regeneration—startling precisely because the concept of the Word of God as a mediate or second cause of regeneration is so widely accepted within the reformed tradition. The paradox here is that, once again, Edwards asserts the instrumentality of means, but also denies the causal efficacy of them; in short, the paradox here is that, effectively, means are not means, that means are not causes, indeed, that (as Malebranche insists) causes are not causes. Edwards explicitly denies here the reality of second causes in the act of regeneration. His emphasis upon the First Cause is such that it effectively swallows up the efficacy and the reality of second causes, and it raises the specter of an occasionalism in the realm of the will.

It will be evident that there is a parallel here between Edwards's views in the sphere of the will and his views in the sphere of God and the creation. More precisely, there is a tantalizing parallel between Edwards's denial of mechanism in the sphere of God and the creation and his denial of means in the sphere of the will. We have already noted that, on the one hand, there is, on Edwards's part, a denial of mechanism—he refers to "that folly of seeking for a mechanical cause of gravity"; he also makes this observation: "therefore we may infallibly conclude that the very being, and the manner of being, and the whole of bodies depends immediately on the divine power."[82] On the other hand, there is, on his part, an assertion of mechanism: "this has as much a mechanical cause as anything in the world, and is as philosophically to be solved, and ought no more to be attributed to the immediate operation of God than everything else."[83] Similarly, we note that, on the one hand, there is, in Edwards's thought, an assertion of means in the realm of grace: "God makes use of means";[84] "but God influences persons

81. Edwards, *Sermons and Discourses, 1730–1733*, 416.

82. Edwards, *Scientific and Philosophical Writings*, 235.

83. Edwards, *Scientific and Philosophical Writings*, 234.

84. Edwards, *Sermons and Discourses, 1730–1733*, 416.

by means."[85] On the other hand, there is, on his part, a denial of means: "There are not truely [*sic*] any second causes of it; . . . The Word of God is no proper cause of this effect."[86] Thus, as with mechanism, so with means, the question cannot be evaded: Does Edwards really believe in means, or not? If so, what exactly do means signify for Edwards? Does his emphasis upon divine immediacy effectively preclude means? What place is there in Edwards's system for second causes? Can means and immediacy truly be reconciled in his system? There can be little doubt that Edwards's stated position in this very significant sermon effectively involves an occasionalism in the realm of soteriology.

The intriguing feature here is that remarkably in this sermon, Edwards divulges this occasionalist strand in his thinking to the people of Northampton. We have already noted the plausible hypothesis that, in general, Edwards tends to deal with issues at two different levels—that he generally makes a distinction between "thinking with the learned" and "speaking with the vulgar"—between speaking in "a strict and philosophical sense" and speaking "in a loose and popular sense"? What is so remarkable about *A Divine and Supernatural Light* is that Edwards appears to make a slight exception to his general rule. In this sermon, he appears to be thinking *and* speaking in "a strict and philosophical sense" with those that might be deemed to be "the vulgar"; namely, his own congregation in Northampton!

THE ADVOCACY OF THE USE OF MEANS

What precisely then is Edwards's view of means in the realm of the will? In view of the fact that there is, in Edwards's thought, a *de facto* (that which is/in fact) suppression of the concept of second causes, mechanism, and means, it is important to note that Edwards has no brief at all for the formal neglect of "the appointed means of grace."[87] Indeed, he clearly regards such a neglect as a manifestation of enthusiasm: "And to expect that the Spirit of God will savingly operate upon their minds, without the Spirit's making use of means, as subservient to the effect, is enthusiastical."[88] It is important to note that Edwards does not despise or belittle the use of means in the matter of regeneration or conversion; indeed, his emphasis upon the use of means in the sphere of the will—the Word of God, preaching, prayer, an earnest seeking after God—is often considerable. "It is most likely," insists Edwards

85. Edwards, *Sermons and Discourses, 1734–38*, 283.

86. Edwards, *Sermons and Discourses, 1730–1733*, 416.

87. Edwards, *Religious Affections*, 138.

88. Edwards, *Religious Affections*, 138.

with regard to saving grace, "that God should bestow this gift in a way of earnest attention to divine truth, and the use of the means of grace."[89] "God influences persons by means."[90] Indeed, D. Bruce Hindmarsh has argued that, over against the tendency towards passivity found in Hyper-Calvinistic circles, Edwards's writings and his example led to the affirmation, within English evangelicalism, of "a larger role for human agency in evangelism and salvation."[91] It is part of the paradox of Jonathan Edwards that he is at one and the same time—or (perhaps we should say) often at different times—the champion of both immediacy and mediacy. The great irony here is that Jonathan Edwards, the great suppressor of the notional concept of means, is also, at one and the same time, the great advocate of the actual use of means.

How, then, are we to reconcile the enormous emphasis upon immediacy in his work as a whole and the powerful emphasis upon means and mechanism elsewhere in his work? Edwards's pivotal statement in *A Divine and Supernatural Light*—"God makes use of means; but it is not as mediate causes to produce this effect. There are not truely [*sic*] any second causes of it; but it is produced by God immediately. The Word of God is no proper cause of this effect"—appears to provide further corroboratory proof of the thesis that the means of grace (the Word of God; the preaching of the word; prayer) are construed not so much as the efficient cause of regeneration or conversion—indeed, the means of grace are not even construed by Edwards as second causes—but rather are construed as connected with or conjoined to this great spiritual change. Thus, just as in the sphere of God and the creation mechanism is construed by Edwards as "the stated method or the stated condition of God's acting," so in the sphere of the will, the means of grace are effectively construed as "the stated method or the stated condition of God's acting."[92] Indeed, the parallel in these two very different spheres demonstrates a very interesting consistency of thought on Edwards's part; there is a sense, however, in which that very consistency highlights the fact that, in Edwards's thought, both mechanism and means are, in their respective spheres, something of an illusion.

89. Hickman, *Works of Jonathan Edwards*, 2.543.

90. Edwards, *Sermons and Discourses, 1734–38*, 283.

91. Hindmarsh, *Edwards at Home and Abroad*, 216.

92. I am indebted to Paul Helm for the observation that, in *Freedom of the Will*, Edwards appears to distinguish implicitly between that which is efficiently caused by *x* and that which is connected with or conjoined to *x*.

THE ANTI-DEISTIC STRAIN

Moreover, it is important to pose this crucial question: If, as is evidently the case, Edwards's emphasis upon divine immediacy is significantly muted in *Freedom of the Will*, is it nevertheless the case that the anti-deistic strain, which clearly constitutes the driving force behind his otherwise very powerful emphasis upon divine immediacy, is still significantly present in this work? In other words, are the theological ends for which Edwards emphasizes divine immediacy elsewhere prominently present in the essay? The answer to these questions is, we believe, decidedly in the affirmative. Edwards's target in the essay is, quite simply, Arminianism. It is important to note, however, that, for Edwards, Arminianism is a very broad, general term that encompasses, as he suggests in the essay itself, "Pelagians, semi-Pelagians, Jesuits, Socinians, Arminians, and others."[93] The question that now arises is this: What is the common denominator in these various schemes? The answer surely is that, in contradistinction to Calvinism, these schemes are all characterized by a relatively higher view of humanity and by a relatively lower view of the work of the Spirit of God; they are all schemes which, in varying degrees, magnify the role played by humanity and reduce the role played by the Spirit. "The term 'Arminianism' then," insists Clyde A. Holbrook, "must be left to stand for a complex of notions involving an elevated confidence in freedom of choice, a sharply upward revised estimate of human nature, and a form of commonsense moralism, all of which were related to an acute dissatisfaction with Calvinism."[94] The Calvinistic scheme scrupulously excludes all human autonomy; these other schemes, in varying degrees, scrupulously include it.

It is significant that in *Freedom of the Will*, Edwards also specifically refers to "our late freethinkers"[95]—those that he describes, in ironic and sardonic vein, as "gentlemen possessed of that noble and generous freedom of thought, which happily prevails in this age of light and inquiry."[96] "Freethinker" was, as *The Oxford English Dictionary* makes clear, "a designation claimed especially by the deistic and other rejectors of Christianity at the beginning of the eighteenth century."[97] The anti-deistic strain of *Freedom of the Will* is clearly incontrovertible; indeed, Edwards specifically refers in

93. Edwards, *Freedom of the Will*, 203.
94. Edwards, *Original Sin*, 4.
95. Edwards, *Freedom of the Will*, 439.
96. Edwards, *Freedom of the Will*, 437.
97. *Oxford English Dictionary*, 2nd ed., s.v. "freethinker."

the essay to "Dr. Samuel Clarke," "Dr. Whitby," and "Dr. Turnbull" as among "the chief of the Arminian writers."[98]

SAMUEL CLARKE (1675–1729)

Samuel Clarke, for his part, was a prominent clergyman-theologian in the Church of England who, in 1704–05, had delivered the Boyle lectures on *The Being and Attributes of God.* He is described by G.R. Cragg as "perhaps the greatest exponent"[99] of the latitudinarian position. A convinced Newtonian, Clarke was essentially deistic in tendency—a rationalist whose exaltation of humanity's innate powers went hand in hand with a derogation of the deity and the glory of the Spirit of God. In 1712, he had published *The Scripture Doctrine of the Trinity.* This work constituted a significant landmark in the Trinitarian Controversy which had broken out in England in the 1690s. "In this seminal work," observes Kenneth P. Minkema, "Clarke renounced the Athanasian Creed's formulation of three co-equal and co-eternal persons as unscriptural and treated the trinitarian question as non-essential to the faith."[100] Indeed, Clarke is a classic contemporary demonstration of the principle that Pelagianism, as a system, coheres with anti-Trinitarianism.

DANIEL WHITBY (1638–1726)

In the course of *Freedom of the Will,* Edwards also turns his attention to the Anglican divine, "Dr. Whitby." "Ranked as an Arminian," observes Paul Ramsey, "Daniel Whitby soon went beyond this position. Apparently, he was much shaken by the views of Samuel Clarke upon our Lord's deity, . . . and his 'retractation,' published 'by his express order' posthumously, evidences an Arian and unitarian tendency."[101] Edwards adds:

> I am sensible, the Doctor's aim in these assertions is against the Calvinists; to shew, in opposition to them, that there is no need of any physical operation of the Spirit of God on the will, to change and determine that to a good choice, but that God's operation and assistance is only moral, suggesting ideas to the understanding.[102]

98. Edwards, *Freedom of the Will*, 217.
99. Cragg, *Age of Reason*, 158.
100. Edwards, *Sermons and Discourses, 1723–1729*, 43n3.
101. Edwards, *Freedom of the Will*, 82.
102. Edwards, *Freedom of the Will*, 220.

By "physical operation of the Spirit of God on the will," Edwards means, presumably, a personal, irresistible, supernatural operation by the Holy Spirit upon humanity's will.[103] This Whitby denied:

> It therefore can be only requisite, in order to these ends, that the good Spirit should so illuminate our understandings, that we attending to, and considering what lies before us, should apprehend, and be convinced of our duty; and that the blessings of the gospel should be so propounded to us, as that we may discern them to be our chiefest good.[104]

Whitby effectively reduces the Spirit's role in conversion to that of a Teacher, the Spirit's work in conversion to that of moral suasion, and the work of conversion itself to that of the sinner's embracing the greatest apparent good, as more or less in any ordinary act of volition—as Edwards expresses it, "that God's operation and assistance is only moral, suggesting ideas to the understanding." Whitby's tacit anthropology here is Pelagian. We note once again the crucial connection between Pelagianism on the one hand and a suppression of the role of the person and work of the Spirit of God on the other.

In his Miscellany "Concerning Efficacious Grace" Edwards returns to a consideration of Dr. Whitby's Arminianizing views of the Spirit of God:

> According to Dr. Whitby's notion of the assistance of the Spirit, the Spirit of God does nothing in the hearts or minds of men beyond the power of the DEVIL, nothing but what the devil can [do] and nothing showing any greater power in any respect than the devil shows and exercises in his temptations. For he supposes that all the Spirit of God does is to bring moral maxims and inducements to mind, and to set 'em before the understanding, etc.[105]

> Dr. Whitby seems to deny any physical influence at all of the Spirit of God on the will, but only *moral suasion*, moral causes . . . Here to show, if God does do anything physically, what he does must be efficacious and irresistible.[106]

Edwards's comparison here between "Dr. Whitby's notion of the assistance of the Spirit" and "the power of the devil" is very interesting. Edwards views Whitby's notions concerning the Spirit as a kind of positive counterpart to

103. Strobel, *Jonathan Edwards's Theology*, 180–81, 204–05.

104. Edwards, *Freedom of the Will*, 219.

105. Edwards, *Writings on the Trinity*, 294.

106. Edwards, *Writings on the Trinity*, 207.

the devil's negative operation on the souls of humanity. "For he supposes that all that the Spirit of God does, is to bring moral motives and inducements to mind, and set 'em before the understanding, etc" Thus, just as the devil sets before the mind temptations, enticements, allurements, in short, incentives of a negative and evil character, so the Spirit, in Whitby's theology, sets before the mind motives, incentives, moral inducements, spiritual allurements and enticements of a positive and holy character. In all of this there is no physical, personal, supernatural operation of the Spirit upon the soul—only an influence by moral suasion and moral causes. Once again, we note that there is here, in the final analysis, no real difference in Whitby's theology between the operation of the Spirit upon the souls of humanity and the operation of motives in general upon the minds of humanity in the established course of things. Whitby's theology of the Spirit here is such that it puts the Third Person of the Godhead at a distance and effectively reduces his person and work to that of a mere moral influence.

In the course of his *Miscellanies* Edwards poses a very significant series of questions with regard to the nature of saving grace:

> The controversy, as it relates to efficacious grace in this sense, includes in it these four questions:
>
> 1. Whether saving virtue differs from common virtue, or such virtue as they [have] that are not in a state of salvation, in nature and kind or only in degree and circumstances?
> 2. Whether a holy disposition of heart, as an internal governing principle of life and practice, be immediately implanted or infused in the soul, or only be contracted by repeated acts and obtained by human culture and improvements?
> 3. Whether conversion, or the change of a person from being a vicious or wicked man to a truly virtuous character, be instantaneous or gradual?
> 4. Whether the divine assistance or influence by which men may obtain true and saving virtue be sovereign and arbitrary, or whether God, in giving this assistance and its effects, limits himself to certain exact and stated rules revealed in his Word and established by his promises?[107]

Edwards's great concern in this controversy between Calvinism and the broad, general, quasi-deistic Arminianism that he opposes is to maintain the immediate, sovereign, supernatural character of regeneration.

107. Edwards, *Writings on the Trinity*, 301–02.

"Regeneration," observes Michael J. McClymond, "is the epistemological foundation of Edwards's entire religious outlook."[108] Thus in this passage, Edwards establishes a sustained, implicit contrast between "common virtue" and "saving virtue," between the natural and the supernatural, between that which is of humanity and that which is of God, between the gradual and the instantaneous, between the mediate and the immediate. He is concerned to demonstrate that the difference between these two kinds of virtue is not a difference in degree, but a fundamental difference in kind. Edwards insists continually upon the immediacy of God in regeneration or conversion, over against the gradualism of the Arminian scheme, and this is a theme to which he constantly returns:

> That the power, and grace, and operation of the Holy Spirit, in, or towards, the conversion of a sinner, is immediate; that the habit of true virtue or holiness is immediately implanted or infused; that the operation goes so far, that a man has habitual holiness given him instantly, wholly by the operation of the Spirit of God, and not gradually by assistance concurring with our endeavours, so as gradually to advance virtue into a prevailing habit.[109]

We have already noted, in the context of God's atemporality, that the concept of divine immediacy enjoys an interesting *double entendre*. The word "immediate" denotes that which is *without time;* it also denotes that which is *without means*. We have noted, moreover, the causal, semantic connection between these two meanings of the word. That connection can be summarized thus: *no means; no time*. We have noted that God's knowledge is immediate both in the sense that it is non-sequential and in the sense that it is non-inferential. We note the same fascinating ambiguity in the concept of divine immediacy as it relates to the doctrine of regeneration. The divine act of the regeneration of the sinner is immediate both in the sense that it is non-gradual and in the sense that it is means-less. There is a great emphasis in Edwards's writings upon the instantaneousness of regeneration, and it is with regard to this very issue that, in his *Miscellanies*, Edwards turns his attention to "Dr. Turnbull."

GEORGE TURNBULL (1698–1748)

George Turnbull was a Scottish moral philosopher who sought ordination in the Anglican Church. In 1740, he published *The Principles of Moral and*

108. McClymond, *Encounters with God*, 111.

109. Hickman, *Works of Jonathan Edwards*, 2.552.

Christian Philosophy, which, notes Peter J. Thuesen, "argued against the Calvinist-Augustinian notion of original sin."[110] In his interaction with the Scottish philosopher, Edwards notes in his *Miscellanies* that Turnbull seeks to explain away "the sudden conversions that were in the apostles' days" as if they were miracles—as if, in short, they were the exception rather than the rule. The rule, for Turnbull, was that of gradual conversions. Edwards's resistance to "this gradual way [of conversion] by contracted habits by Greek culture [*sic*], as Turnbull speaks of"[111] is very significant. To assert the gradual was, obviously, to deny the immediate, and to deny the immediate was to assert the mediate—it was to assert the potentially intrinsic efficacy of means. It was to deny a supernatural, divine act and to turn it into a more or less natural, human process that, for Turnbull and others, consisted of diligence, culture, and contracted habits. "Turnbull," notes Edwards in his *Miscellanies*, "speaks of good men as 'born again,' i.e. changed by culture."[112] It is precisely because Edwards lived in an age in which "common virtue" was being subtly and dangerously confused with "saving virtue" that he emerges constantly as the inveterate opponent of all Arminian gradualism. Indeed, it is evident that Edwards regarded the issue of divine immediacy as a kind of theological litmus test that both vindicated and safeguarded the divine, sovereign, supernatural, and irresistible character of regeneration.

Man's inveterate tendency to put and to keep God at a distance, even in the midst of his religious schemes, was clearly a profound preoccupation of the New England divine. This tendency was, for Edwards, humanity's foolish, sinful counterblast to the immediacy of God. In his *Treatise on Grace,*[113] written, it appears, in the early 1740s, Edwards makes this significant general statement:

> No good reason can be given why men should have such an inward disposition to deny any immediate communication between God and the creature, or to make as little of it as possible. 'Tis a strange disposition that men have to thrust God out of the world, or to put him as far out of sight as they can, and to have in no respect immediately and sensibly to do with him. Therefore so many schemes have been drawn to exclude, or extenuate, or remove at a great distance, any influence of the Divine Being

110. Edwards, *Catalogue of Books*, 48.

111. Edwards, *Writings on the Trinity*, 296.

112. Edwards, *Writings on the Trinity*, 297.

113. This work was published posthumously in 1865. See Edwards, *Writings on the Trinity*, 149–52.

in the hearts of men, such as the scheme of the Pelagians, the Socinians, etc.[114]

ARMINIAN GRADUALISM

In the course of his *Treatise on Grace,* Edwards insists once again upon the immediacy of God in the work of conversion; such immediacy, he insists, necessarily involves instantaneousness. Edwards notes that the work of conversion is represented in the Scriptures by both the act of creation and the act of raising the dead, each of which is, by definition, characterized by instantaneousness: "In creation, something is brought out of nothing in an instant. God speaks and it is done; he commands and it stands fast. When the dead are raised, it is done in a moment."[115] Edwards's manifest concern in emphasizing "the instantaneousness of the work of conversion"[116] is, again, that of opposing what he regards as the pernicious gradualism of the Arminian scheme:

> Hence we may learn that it is impossible for men to convert themselves by their own strength and industry, with only a concurring assistance helping in the exercise of their natural abilities and principles of the soul, and securing their improvement. For what is gained after this manner is a gradual acquisition, and not something instantaneously begotten, and of an entirely different nature, and wholly of a separate kind, from all that was in the nature of the person the moment before. All that men can do by their own strength and industry is only gradually to increase and improve and new-model and direct qualities, principles and perfections of nature that they have already.[117]

Kyle C. Strobel observes:

> In *Divine Light,* Edwards follows Owen, Mastricht and Turretin in emphasizing the *immediacy* of the Spirit's work in the soul. This account pushes against the idea of "moral suasion," that God somehow works externally to coax the unregenerate to regenerate. For Edwards, this is impossible. Regeneration entails a

114. Edwards, *Writings on the Trinity*, 177.

115. Edwards, *Writings on the Trinity*, 161.

116. Edwards, *Writings on the Trinity*, 162.

117. Edwards, *Writings on the Trinity*, 164.

> new creation, a new nature, and not merely an additional power added to the faculties.[118]

The significance of the concept of the immediacy of God in the work of regeneration lies, therefore, in the fact that, over against the moralizing, ethicizing tendency of the age, it protects the doctrine of regeneration or conversion from any potential reduction into a mere modification of natural attributes and qualities, and thus safeguards the divine, sovereign, supernatural nature of that work.

ABSOLUTE DEPENDENCE

We have noted that, in the sphere of "God and the Creation," Edwards emphasizes that the dependence of the cosmos upon God is a moment-by-moment dependence; this category of dependence coheres supremely with his occasionalism. We note also that, here, in the sphere of "the will," Edwards emphasizes that the dependence of the sinner upon the God of salvation is an entire, absolute, and universal dependence; this category of dependence coheres supremely with his Calvinism. This latter category is the central theme of the lecture, *God Glorified in the Work of Redemption, by the Greatness of Man's Dependence upon Him in the Whole of it* (1731). The text on which the lecture was based was First Corinthians 1:29–31: "That no flesh should glory in his presence . . . [T]hat, according as it is written, he that glorieth, let him glory in the Lord." In this lecture, Edwards states the following as his doctrine: "God is glorified in the wisdom of redemption in this, that there appears in it so absolute and universal a dependence of the redeemed on him."[119] Both title and text indicate the crucial connection, in Edwards's mind, between the concept of the dependence of humanity and the concept of the glory of God. It should be noted that there is, in Edwards's thought, a fascinating parallel between his rejection of the concept of cosmic autonomy and his rejection of the concept of human autonomy. This lecture, delivered in Boston during the week of the Commencement at Harvard, constituted, therefore, a major, early blow in what Kenneth P. Minkema has described as "an ideological and theological civil war that would occupy nearly his entire life";[120] namely, his battle with Arminianism.

118. Strobel, *Reinterpretation*, 180–81.

119. Edwards, *Sermons and Discourses, 1730–1733*, 202.

120. Edwards, *Sermons and Discourses, 1730–1733*, 8. Wilson H. Kimnach makes the observation, in the context of the "Great Apostasy" at Yale in 1722, that "J.E. was determined to stand for the New England Way, and anti-Arminianism seems to have become his banner." Edwards, *Sermons and Discourses, 1720–1723*, 287n7.

Absolute sovereignty, absolute dependence—these are the dual emphases of the lecture. Thus all putative human autonomy is just as insistently and emphatically excluded from Edwards's system as all putative cosmic autonomy. There is an unashamed absoluteness and a totalitarianism about the theology of Jonathan Edwards—an absoluteness and a totalitarianism that appear, in Edwards's mind, to constitute the essential *sine qua non* of the maximal glory of God.

The following passage in the section of the lecture, entitled "Use," demonstrates that Edwards clearly had Arminianism and its correlates in view:

> Hence those doctrines and schemes of divinity that are in any respect opposite to such an absolute and universal dependence on God, do derogate from God's glory, and thwart the design of the contrivance of our redemption. Those schemes that put the creature in God's stead, in any of the mentioned respects, that exalt man into the place of either Father, Son, or Holy Ghost, in anything pertaining to our redemption; that however they may allow of a dependence of the redeemed on God, yet deny a dependence that is so absolute and universal; that own an entire dependence on God for some things, but not for others; that own that we depend on God for the gift and acceptance of a redeemer, but deny so absolute a dependence on him for the obtaining of an interest in the Redeemer; that own an absolute dependence on the Father for giving his Son, and on the Son for working out redemption, but not so entire a dependence on the Holy Ghost for conversion, and a being in Christ, and so coming to a title to his benefits; that own a dependence on God for means of grace, but not absolutely for the benefit and success of those means; that own a partial dependence on the power of God, for the obtaining and exercising holiness, but not a mere dependence on the arbitrary and sovereign grace of God; . . . and whatever other way any scheme is inconsistent with our entire dependence on God for all, and in each of those ways, of having all *of* him, *through* him, and *in* him, it is repugnant to the design and tenor of the gospel, and robs it of that which God accounts its luster and glory.[121]

Edwards's reasoning in *God Glorified* is that there is a crucial connection between anthropology and the doctrine of the Trinity. His tacit position can be summarized thus: a low view of human ability coheres with a high view of the Spirit; thus Calvinism, as a system, coheres with Trinitarianism. Conversely, a high view of human ability coheres with a low view of the

121. Edwards, *Sermons and Discourses, 1730–1733*, 212–13.

Spirit; thus Pelagianism, as a system, coheres with Unitarianism.[122] It is for this reason that we find throughout the whole corpus of Edwards's writings a colossal emphasis both upon original sin and upon the supernatural influences of the Spirit of God. Thus, in the final analysis, Arminianism, whether Semi-Pelagian or Pelagian, displays a relative independence from the Holy Spirit and is, therefore, intrinsically subversive of the doctrine of the Trinity. It is precisely because Arminianism subverts the role, and thus the absolute sovereignty, of the Spirit of God that it is corrosive of the doctrine of the deity of the Spirit. As far as Edwards was concerned, the tendency of Arminianism was essentially anti-trinitarian and thus essentially Unitarian or deistic.

Mark Valeri notes, in the Boston lecture of 1731, this logical connection between Calvinism and Trinitarianism on the one hand and between Arminianism and anti-trinitarianism on the other hand:

> The central theme of *God Glorified* is the dependence of fallen humanity on all three persons of the Trinity for salvation . . . Those who judge human beings to be not completely depraved grant them independence from God, deny the need for either the Son or the Spirit, and therefore, by implication, reject the Godhead. Any concession to human ability, such as is made by Arminians, amounts to unbelief. Conversely, a doctrine of sin in Calvinist fashion affirms humanity's need for all persons of the Trinity and therefore glorifies God.[123]

> Edwards defends the Calvinist view of human nature by linking it to the doctrine of the Trinity . . . By implication, Arminian views on human nature, which deny humanity's complete dependence on God, effectively contradict the logic of the Trinity.[124]

Edwards's insistence upon the entire and absolute dependence of humanity upon God in the matter of redemption coheres with his insistence upon the immediacy of God. Humanity's natural tendency is to assert their independence from God, to distance themselves from God and to distance God from themselves. This tendency is evident not only in humanity's theology (the deistic tendency), but also in their anthropology-*cum*-soteriology (the Pelagian tendency). This latter tendency is found in those Arminianizing schemes which, as Edwards expresses it above in *God Glorified*, "exalt man

122. We are dealing here with the issue of humanity as sinful, not with the issue of humanity made in the image of God.

123. Edwards, *Sermons and Discourses, 1730–1733*, 35–6.

124. Edwards, *Sermons and Discourses, 1730–1733*, 196, 199.

into the place of either Father, Son, or Holy Ghost," that "put the creature in God's stead." There is a connection in Edwards's thought between the dependence-theme and the distance-theme. Dependence upon God involves proximity, and absolute dependence involves the closest proximity; it is the Calvinist who insists upon this absolute dependence. Conversely, independence from God—whether relative or absolute—involves distance, or rather distancing; it is the Arminian that insists upon this relative independence. Indeed, the atheist, the deist, the non-Christian, the nominal Christian, the Arminian—each of these, in different ways and in varying degrees, asserts his independence from God and thus distances himself from God. Edwards clearly sees humanity as constantly pushing God away from themselves. They love independence and they hate dependence; they love the darkness and they hate the light; they love the distance and they hate proximity.

LIBERTARIANISM

This inveterate tendency in humanity to distance God from themselves and to distance themselves from God is a very significant element in Edwards's implacable opposition to the Libertarian and Arminian notion of what he describes as "the self-determining power of the will." This notion insisted that such is the power inherently possessed by the will that, at the point where a free agent chooses *A*, they might also have chosen *NOT-A* or *B*. This is the putative sovereignty possessed by humanity's will. Pivotal to this supposed sovereignty on the part of the will are the related notions of indifference or equilibrium. In this situation, the mind is supposedly poised *in equilibrio* (in equilibrium) in such a way that there is no antecedent bias or preponderation and it might just as easily choose either alternative; indeed, this libertarian position is also known as "alternativity." The theological ramifications of this position, as evidenced by Arminianism, are obvious: If, as Libertarians and Arminians maintained, humanity's will is marked by a sovereignty over itself, then this sovereignty pits itself against the sovereignty of God; it effectively destroys the absolute sovereignty of God; there is no such thing as irresistible grace, and humanity is able to push God away, to push God around, and to keep God at bay as and when they please. This, then, is the rationale for Edwards's profound philosophical and theological antipathy to the concept of the self-determining power of the will. Once human autonomy is conceded, then also conceded is the notion that sinners can close with Christ when and where they please, or can just as easily not close with him at all. Thus the concept of "the self-determining power of the will" is one which, by definition, keeps God at bay—it keeps God at a distance, waiting on the sidelines, as it were, and it only allows him access and entry as and when "the willer" sees fit.

Indeed, it is evident from Edwards's statement in *Freedom of the Will* that he regarded Arminianizing schemes not only as asserting humanity's independence from God, but also as essentially inverting the *de jure* (that which ought to be the case) humanity-dependent-upon-God relationship into a *de facto* God-dependent-upon-humanity relationship. The Scriptures represent God as the King of kings, the Lord of lords, the God of gods, as the Most High God who does what he wills in the counsels of heaven, as the great God who reigns and rules over the kingdoms of humanity—and none can stay his hand. God is the absolute sovereign of the universe—God is the potter and humanity is the clay. This is the *de jure* humanity-dependent-upon-God concept found in the Scriptures and in Calvinism. But Arminianism inverts this and represents God as if he were a kind of glorified waiter, one who stands, as it were, at humanity's beck and call, simply waiting for humanity's nod; so that, if humanity says, "Come," God comes, and if humanity says, "Go," God goes. In effect, humanity is the potter and God the clay. This is the absurd *de facto* God-dependent-upon-humanity notion found in Libertarianism and Arminianism—God is put at a distance and is effectively reduced to the status of a divine waiter.

The analogy utilized by Edwards in his *Miscellanies* to illustrate the absurdity of the Arminian position is, of course, not that of the waiter; it is that of "a skilful mariner," as in the following cogent *reductio ad absurdum* (reduction to the point of absurdity) of the concept of "the self-determining power of the will":

> If God does not some way in his providence, and so in his predeterminations, order what the volitions of men shall be, he would be as dependent in governing the world, as a skilful mariner is in governing his ship, in passing over a turbulent, tempestuous ocean, where he meets constantly, and through the whole voyage, with things that agitate the ship, have great influence on the motions of it, and are so cross and grievous to him that he is obliged to accommodate himself in the best manner that he can. He meets with cross winds, violent tempests, strong currents, and great opposition from enemies; none of which things he has the disposal of, but is forced to suffer. He only guides the ship, and, by his skill, turns that hither and thither, and steers it in such a manner as to avoid dangers, as well as the case will allow.[125]

125. Hickman, *Works of Jonathan Edwards*, 2.539.

Such, then, is the essentially helpless, hapless passivity and vulnerability of the God of Arminianism—such a God "is obliged to accommodate himself in the best manner that he can," "as well as the case will allow." This dreadfully debased, degraded conception of God is the *reductio ad absurdum* of the Libertarian and Arminian notion of the sovereign self-determining power of the will. It is precisely this *de facto* God-dependent-upon-humanity notion that was anathema to Jonathan Edwards. The Arminian view of God's redemption, he insists in *Freedom of the Will*, "is truly repugnant to the absolute sovereignty of God, and inconsistent with the supremacy of his will; and really subjects the will of the most High to the will of his creatures, and brings him into dependence upon them."[126] It is precisely this *de jure* humanity-absolutely-dependent-upon-God principle that was utterly sacrosanct with Edwards. The God of Edwards is, as he himself insists in *Freedom of the Will*, "the supreme and absolute Governor of the universe,"[127] "the all-wise determiner of all events,"[128] and "the supreme orderer of all things."[129] He is a God marked by "absolute sovereignty," the counterpart of which is "absolute dependence" on the part of humanity. What is so interesting in Edwards is that he appears to seek to enhance the concept of the "absolute sovereignty" of God (if that were possible) via his enormous emphasis upon the immediacy of God. This fact emerges supremely perhaps in his thinking on "God and the Creation"; but it is also discernible in his thinking on "the Will." Each of these realms is marked by a distinct suppression of second causes, and thus by a definite occasionalism. Edwards's principal concern in the realm of "the Will," however, is, it appears, to establish the divinity, the supernaturalism, and the immediacy of the regeneration of the sinner over against the naturalism, the mediacy, and the gradualism of the deistic, Pelagianizing tendencies of the age. Indeed, there can be little doubt that Jonathan Edwards regarded the issue of the immediacy of God in the regeneration of humanity as a crucial citadel in the great battle with the rationalizing, naturalizing, and moralizing impulse of the early and mid-eighteenth-century Enlightenment.

126. Edwards, *Freedom of the Will*, 396.

127. Edwards, *Freedom of the Will*, 404.

128. Edwards, *Freedom of the Will*, 410.

129. Edwards, *Freedom of the Will*, 411.

ECCLESIOLOGY

A SILENT REVOLUTION

It is a fact of great interest that, contemporaneously with the revolution that was unleashed in the scientific world of Old England by the publication of Newton's *Principia* in 1687, there was unfolding in the ecclesiastical world of New England a revolution of a very different kind. "This silent revolution,"[1] as Edmund S. Morgan aptly describes it, was a revolution that related not to the physical world and the intellectual realm, but to the spiritual world and the ecclesiastical realm. It had to do with the increased availability of the sacrament of baptism in the Congregational churches of New England; before long it also had to do with the increased availability of the sacrament of the Lord's Supper. Each of these revolutions, whether the Newtonian revolution in the realm of science or "this silent revolution" in the realm of the church, was to have very significant ramifications with regard to the issue of the immediacy of God. If the former revolution had the effect of distancing God from the cosmos, the latter revolution had the effect of distancing God from the church. Indeed, in the name of making God, via the sacraments, more accessible to the people, it actually introduced into the church innovative mechanisms, the net effect of which was that of pushing God away and keeping God at arm's length.

"THE NEW ENGLAND EXPERIMENT"

How then did "this silent revolution" occur, and what was the essence of it? "The New England experiment" of the 1630s and 40s was, of course, rooted

1. Morgan, *Visible Saints*, 145.

in the ideal of ecclesiastical purity—a purity that expressed itself in exclusiveness. "The English emigrants to New England," notes Morgan, "were the first Puritans to restrict membership in the church to visible saints."[2] The intention was not merely that of excluding the visibly wicked, but also that of excluding the visibly good, if unregenerate. Thus both the civil and the uncivil were, on principle, to be kept out of the church, if unconverted; it was as visible saints that men must qualify for membership of the church of Christ. "In moving their churches so close to God and so far from the world," observes Morgan, "the New England Puritans were doing what they believed that God required."[3] For the New England Puritan mind, ecclesiastical purity was the necessary prerequisite for proximity to and intimacy with God.

The problem that arose in New England Congregationalism in the 1640s and 50s lay in the tension that is almost inevitably found in paedobaptist ecclesiology between the continuities of family life and the discontinuities of saving faith; it was, as Morgan expresses it, "the problem of biology,"[4] or "the problem of the next generation."[5] This rapidly developing situation is, perhaps, best understood in terms of three successive generations within the churches. The first generation consisted of believers from overseas who had, let us say, arrived in New England as part of the Great Migration of the 1630s; these believers were already baptized and continued to have access to the sacrament of the Lord's Supper. The second generation consisted of the covenant children of this first generation; they were baptized, but in many cases did not have access to the Lord's Supper because, although now adult, they had not made a profession of faith in Christ. The third generation consisted of the children of the latter—they were the children of baptized, *prima facie* unbelievers; and the question that inevitably arose with regard to them was whether or not they had a right to baptism.

THE HALFWAY COVENANT

"By the late 1640s," notes Morgan, "an increasing number of children who had been baptized in New England churches were coming of age without a religious experience and starting families of their own. The synod which met at Cambridge from 1646 to 1648 had been asked to decide the status of these persons. Since it failed to do so, every church during the 1650s had to face the question for itself, and most of them seem to have adopted

2. Morgan, *Visible Saints*, 113.
3. Morgan, *Visible Saints*, 114.
4. Morgan, *Visible Saints*, 125.
5. Morgan, *Visible Saints*, 136.

a do-nothing policy by neither expelling the second-generation adults nor baptizing their third-generation children."[6] With the passage of every year, the situation became increasingly urgent, and when a full-scale synod convened in 1662, it delivered *inter alia* the following proposition:

> Proposition 5th. Church-members who were admitted in minority, understanding the Doctrine of Faith, and publickly [*sic*] professing their assent thereto; not scandalous in life, and solemnly owning the Covenant before the Church, wherein they give up themselves and their Children to the Lord, and subject themselves to the Government of Christ in the Church, their Children are to be Baptized.[7]

Such was the ecclesiastical expedient of the Halfway Covenant—the term was originally derisive. It is important to note that this "owning the covenant" on the part of the second generation was designed to fall short of a genuine profession of faith in Christ. This fifth proposition clearly required *notitia* (knowledge) and *assensus* (assent), but was tailored in such a way that it deliberately fell short of an insistence upon the necessity of *fiducia* (trust). Morgan describes the extent and the limitations of the blessings of "halfway membership":

> The membership they retained . . . was the continuation of the membership they had had as children: they could not vote in church affairs, and they could not participate in the Lord's Supper (they were not members in "full communion"). What they gained was two privileges which had probably been hitherto denied them in most New England churches: the application of church discipline (they could be admonished or excommunicated for bad conduct) and baptism for their children. They were "half-way" members.[8]

STODDARDISM

This already complex and unsatisfactory situation was then further complicated and exacerbated by the fact that, in 1677, Edwards's own grandfather, Solomon Stoddard (1643–1729), introduced into the Northampton church the practice of "open communion." Perry Miller notes:

6. Morgan, *Visible Saints*, 129.
7. Cited in Morgan, *Visible Saints*, 130.
8. Morgan, *Visible Saints*, 131–32.

> For five years, Stoddard dutifully kept the customary double-entry ledger. Then, in 1677, without warning, without so much as a by-your-leave, . . . he closed the separate account of baptisms. Thereafter—secure in his Congregational autonomy but still more in his frontier remoteness—he baptized every adult who assented to the articles of faith, and admitted him to the Supper. He treated the congregation and virtually the whole town . . . as the church.[9]

Stoddard justified this innovation on the grounds that the Lord's Supper was, allegedly, "a converting ordinance." Thus, if the Halfway Covenant administered the sacrament of baptism to infants who, strictly speaking, did not qualify as children of the covenant, Stoddardism administered the sacrament of the Lord's Supper to adults who had made no pretension to faith in Christ. The almost-universal availability of both sacraments simply had the effect of cheapening them. This is the great paradox in Stoddard's ministry: On the one hand, Edwards's grandfather preached powerful evangelistic sermons from his Northampton pulpit. On the other hand, in repudiating the concept of the gathered church, he played a pivotal role in introducing into the churches of New England a conception of the church that was much more relaxed, inclusive, and comprehensive than that embraced by the New England churches at the beginning. Stoddard regarded the church as a territorial unit that embraced all professing Christians within it, whether regenerate or unregenerate. Thus the Halfway Covenant had been replaced by a covenant in which full covenantal privileges were now made available to those that did not profess Christ. C.C. Goen makes the interesting observation that "on the eve of the Great Awakening, most of the parish churches in New England, like the old English churches from which they had fled, harbored a mixed company."[10] Indeed, in 1700 Increase Mather predicted that, if Stoddard's views were to gain ground as rapidly in the ensuing thirty years as they had in the preceding thirty, the people of God in New England would have to "gather churches out of churches."[11]

A REVISED ASSESSMENT

David D. Hall has recently provided an interestingly revised interpretation of the developing situation in the churches of New England: "Stoddard's was

9. Miller, *New England Mind*, 227. This does not mean that, under Stoddardism, the baptism of infants ceased.

10. Edwards, *Great Awakening*, 2.

11. Cited in Morgan, *Visible Saints*, 151.

a simple remedy to a messy theological and pastoral situation."[12] His remedy was, Hall contends, "responding to a specific pastoral situation, a spiritual paralysis among lay people troubled by the intertwining of assurance and access to the Lord's Supper."[13] The "spiritual paralysis" to which Hall refers lay, in large part, in a diffidence on the part of the people to relate their spiritual experience:

> The nexus between church membership and spiritual experience added yet another layer of complications. That nexus was forged in New England in the 1630s when most of the clergy agreed to require candidates for church membership to make a relation of spiritual experience—in effect, to describe the work of grace and how it had transformed them into saints.[14]

Indeed, Hall demonstrates this "spiritual paralysis" by means of an interesting statistic:

> By the third quarter of the century a series of compromises or shifts in policy—whether local variations on the halfway covenant or that policy itself—worked to make church membership more inclusive. But as more people gained access to baptism, the number of members in "full communion" steadily decreased. Any generalization is hazardous, but at the time of the Great Awakening the ratio of baptized (or halfway) members to full members encompassed a range that, at one extreme, approached ten to one.[15]

Hall views the innovation of Stoddardism as essentially an expression of "popular religion"[16]—it was "a simple remedy to a messy theological and pastoral situation." There is an important element of truth in this assessment. The Halfway Covenant was essentially a compromise, and the problems inherent in the compromise laid a foundation for further compromise. The exaggerated dichotomy with regard to the sacraments created by the Halfway Covenant; the relative availability of baptism on the one hand and the relative unavailability of the Lord's Supper on the other; the traditional requirement of a relation of the work of grace; the ensuing diffidence, reluctance, and over-scrupulosity on the part of the people with regard to this latter sacrament—these were the factors that contributed to the "spiritual

12. Edwards, *Ecclesiastical Writings*, 40.
13. Edwards, *Ecclesiastical Writings*, 43.
14. Edwards, *Ecclesiastical Writings*, 34.
15. Edwards, *Ecclesiastical Writings*, 36.
16. Edwards, *Ecclesiastical Writings*, 44.

paralysis" evident in the people of New England. Hall rejects the notion that Stoddardism promoted laxity, declension, and hypocrisy. "Stoddardeanism," he insists, "did not turn the townspeople into hypocrites."[17]

Hall has unquestionably shed some very important light upon the *de facto* situation in the churches of New England; but Hall's fundamental thesis is unconvincing. We do not deny, nor did Edwards, the obviously powerful evangelistic character of the ministry of Solomon Stoddard. The problem is that there is clearly an inherent inconsistency, indeed, a major inherent contradiction, between Stoddard's soteriology on the one hand and his ecclesiology on the other. Indeed, a powerful case can be made that his ecclesiology had an intrinsic tendency to undermine his soteriology. If his soteriology can be said to have brought men nigh to God, his ecclesiology can be said to have pushed God away. Stoddard's position was clearly out of harmony with the classic New England Puritan position; indeed, with its emphasis upon the territorial nature of the church and its willingness to contemplate the church as "a mixed multitude," it was, in fact, albeit inadvertently perhaps, a classic Anglican position.

It is vital to understand that Edwards's ultimate position with regard to the Lord's Supper in the late 1740s was, quite simply, a matter of principle. It is all the more important to understand this fact precisely because, significantly, Hall both commences and concludes his "Editor's Introduction" with the assertion that Edwards was "a person of his time and place."[18] Hall tends to over-contextualize, and thus to relativize, Edwards's position; indeed, he fails to understand the absoluteness and the totalitarianism of Edwards's theology. This crucial fact of the principial nature of Edwards's position emerges at the very outset of *An Humble Inquiry into the Rules of the Word of God Concerning . . . Full Communion in the Visible Christian Church* (1749):

> The main question I would consider, and for the negative of which, I would offer some arguments in the following discourse, is this: whether, according to the rules of Christ, any ought to be admitted to the communion and privileges of members of the visible church of Christ in complete standing, but such as are in profession, and in the eye of the church's Christian judgment, godly or gracious persons?[19]

Of paramount importance to Jonathan Edwards in this matter were "the rules of Christ." Edwards's rule of faith and practice was not "the traditions of men"; it was not the doctrine and practice of his grandfather and

17. Edwards, *Ecclesiastical Writings*, 85.
18. Edwards, *Ecclesiastical Writings*, 1, 85.
19. Edwards, *Ecclesiastical Writings*, 174.

predecessor, Solomon Stoddard; it was not "popular religion"; it was not even "The New England Way" of the 1630s. His preeminent concern was, as the title of his treatise demonstrates, with "the rules of the Word of God." For this principle and for this cause Edwards was willing, as the events of 1749–1751 incontestably prove, to stake, as he put it, "my own reputation, future usefulness, and my very subsistence."[20]

Interestingly, Hall takes particular issue with the interpretation of the communion controversy provided by Edwards's great-grandson, Sereno E. Dwight (1786–1850), in the early nineteenth century. "Dwight's thesis," Hall contends, "may be reduced to the phrase, 'Stoddardeanism (i.e. 'laxness') begat Arminianism.'"[21] According to Hall, "Dwight connected two quite different processes and made one the cause of the other. The first of these was an easing of access to church membership that he traced back to the 'half-way covenant' decision of the Synod of 1662."[22] Hall contends that, according to Dwight, Stoddardism simply aided and abetted this trend. But the easing of access to the church accelerated a second process; namely, "a weakening of doctrinal orthodoxy as 'liberals' began to emphasize free will and human ability, a tendency that culminated in the rise of Unitarianism."[23]

THE PURITY OF THE CHURCH

The issue, in the final analysis, is not what Sereno E. Dwight thought, but what Jonathan Edwards thought, and it is very evident from Edwards's own writings on the communion controversy of 1749–1750 that he was convinced that Stoddard's innovations were, in fact, powerfully subversive of the purity of the church of Christ and powerfully conducive to the very laxity, declension, and hypocrisy which Hall denies. In the course of his treatise, Edwards pointedly traces the increasing corruption and degeneracy of the people of Israel; indeed, he draws a pointed parallel between Israel, the Church of England, and the churches of New England. It should be noted that the context of this parallel is that of the hypocrisy of the nation of Israel:

> In succeeding generations, as the people grew more corrupt, I suppose, their covenanting or swearing into the name of the Lord degenerated into a matter of mere form and ceremony; even as subscribing religious articles seems to have done with the Church of England; and as, 'tis to be feared, owning the

20. Edwards, *Ecclesiastical Writings*, 170.
21. Edwards, *Ecclesiastical Writings*, 2.
22. Edwards, *Ecclesiastical Writings*, 2.
23. Edwards, Ecclesiastical Writings, 2.

> covenant, as 'tis called, has too much done in New England; it being visibly a prevailing custom for persons to neglect this, till they come to be married, and then to do it for their credit's sake, and that their children may be baptized. And I suppose, there was commonly a great laxness in Israel among the priests who had the conduct of this affair.[24]

With great candidness, Edwards describes Stoddard's system as "the practice of promiscuous admission"[25]:

> The effect of this method of proceeding in the churches in New England, which have fallen into it, is actually this. There are some that are received into these churches under the notion of their being in the judgment of rational charity visible saints or professing saints, who yet at the same time are actually open professors of heinous wickedness; I mean, the wickedness of living in known impenitence and unbelief, the wickedness of living in enmity against God, and in the rejection of Christ under the gospel.[26]

Thus if, as Edwards contends, "There are some that are received into these churches under the notion of their being in the judgment of rational charity visible saints or professing saints, who yet at the same time are actually open professors of heinous wickedness," is it too much to claim that the system which, in the name of Jesus Christ, promotes such a situation is marked by laxness, declension, and hypocrisy? Indeed, it is a fact that cannot be controverted that Edwards's treatises on the theme of the Lord's Supper are replete with the vocabulary and the concepts of laxness, irregularity, formalism, nominalism, ceremonialism, unbelief, lukewarmness, gracelessness, presumption, show, sham, pretense, absurdity, promiscuity, hypocrisy, deadness, pollution, corruption, declension, degeneracy, and ruin.

THE NECESSITY OF POSITIVE JUDGEMENT

Ever since the introduction of the Halfway Covenant in 1662, the concept of being "not scandalous in life" had played a pivotal and increasing role in the thinking and the practice of the Congregational churches of New England. Stoddard's own innovations in 1677 with regard to the Lord's Supper, in

24. Edwards, *Ecclesiastical Writings*, 213.
25. Edwards, *Ecclesiastical Writings*, 323.
26. Edwards, *Ecclesiastical Writings*, 321.

which he had asserted that ministers "should admit all not scandalous,"[27] strengthened this notion further. In the treatise of 1749, Edwards issued a strong challenge to this by then widely accepted notion:

> When I speak, in the question, of being godly or gracious in the eye of a Christian judgment, by "Christian judgment" I intend something further than a kind of mere negative charity, implying that we forbear to censure and condemn a man, because we don't know but that he may be godly . . . But I mean a positive judgment, founded on some positive appearance, or visibility, some outward manifestations that ordinarily render the thing probable. There is a difference between suspending our judgment, or forbearing to condemn, or having some hope that possibly the thing may be so, and so hoping the best; and a positive judgment in favor of a person.[28]

In his treatise Edwards sets in antithesis "a kind of mere negative charity" and "a positive judgment of charity."[29] His position here is, quite simply, the classic evangelical and Reformed position that it is one thing not to be scandalous; it is quite another thing to be holy. What was required was not simply the absence of scandal, but the presence of repentance and faith. The criterion of being "not scandalous" was a criterion that was obviously conducive to a much greater inclusiveness or comprehensiveness, in short, to what Morgan describes as "a more worldly purity."[30] Thus the concept of the church had shifted startlingly from that of a *de jure* society of believers in Christ to that of a *de facto* community of decent, moral, upright, respectable, quasi-Christian people. The great problem, perhaps the great irony, in Edwards's mind, however, was that unbelief—all too often found in those who are "not scandalous"—was itself a great scandal. Around 1730, Edwards wrote in his *Notes on Scripture* that "unbelief . . . is a great immorality."[31]

THE ISSUE OF SAVING FAITH

The central issue in this controversy for Edwards, then, was the issue of "saving faith," which he describes as "the grand condition of the covenant

27. Morgan, *Visible Saints*, 149.
28. Edwards, *Ecclesiastical Writings*, 178.
29. Edwards, *Ecclesiastical Writings*, 239.
30. Morgan, *Visible Saints*, 150.
31. Edwards, *Notes on Scripture*, 112.

of Christ."[32] For Edwards "saving faith" did not consist merely in *notitia* and *assensus;* it consisted also in *fiducia.* In other words, it did not consist merely in the knowledge of certain historical or doctrinal facts relating to the gospel of Christ and a mental assent to these facts; it also consisted in the consent of the heart and the will:

> To own this covenant, is to profess the consent of our *hearts* to it; and that is the sum and substance of true piety. 'Tis not only a professing of the assent of our understandings, that we understand there is such a covenant, or that we understand we are obliged to comply with it; but 'tis to profess the consent of our wills, it is to manifest *that we do comply with it.* There is mutual profession in this affair, a profession on Christ's part, and a profession on our part; as it is in marriage. And 'tis the same sort of profession that is made on both sides, in this respect, that each professes a consent of heart: Christ in his Word declares an entire consent of heart as to what he offers; and the visible Christian, in the answer that he makes to it in his Christian profession, declares a consent and compliance of heart to his proposal.[33]

Thus Edwards is adamant that "historical faith" is, in the final analysis, no faith at all. Louis Berkhof defines "historical faith" thus:

> This is a purely intellectual apprehension of the truth, devoid of any moral or spiritual purpose . . . It is . . . expressive of the idea that this faith accepts the truths of Scripture as one might accept a history in which one is not personally interested. This faith may be the result of tradition, of education, of public opinion, of an insight into the moral grandeur of Scripture, and so on, accompanied with the general operations of the Holy Spirit. It may be very orthodox and Scriptural, but is not rooted in the heart . . . It is a *fides humana,* and not a *fides divina.*[34]

Edwards makes the following observation with regard to "historical faith" in the context of "the primitive converts to Christianity":

> Indeed, if the faith which they professed in order to baptism, was only a historical or doctrinal faith (as some suppose) or any common faith, it would not have been any visible entering into the covenant of grace; for a common faith is not the condition

32. Edwards, *Ecclesiastical Writings*, 206.
33. Edwards, *Ecclesiastical Writings*, 205.
34. Berkhof, *Systematic Theology*, 501–02.

> of that covenant; . . . but a profession of historical faith implies no profession of accepting Christ as our King, nor engagement to submit to him as such.[35]

The problem with Stoddardism is that it openly and unashamedly sanctioned a mere historical faith; the problem with a mere historical faith is that, far from bringing humanity nigh to God, it actually distances them from God. Historical faith is a detached faith; there is no closing with Christ, there is no "faith of dependence,"[36] and it makes of humanity mere auditors and spectators. Indeed, Edwards himself contrasts true believers with mere auditors and spectators: "By those that hear Christ's sayings, in this place, are not meant merely auditors of the word preached; . . . but those who profess to hearken to, believe and yield submission to the word of Christ."[37] He says elsewhere: "To profess the covenant of grace is to profess the covenant, not as a spectator, but as one immediately concerned in the affair, as a party in the covenant professed."[38] It is interesting to note Edwards's use of the word "immediately" in this context—indeed, his use of the concept of immediacy. The spectator or the auditor is always somewhat detached and at a distance; the participant is always immediately and intimately involved.

PROCRASTINATION

It is at this juncture in his treatise that Edwards deals with another evasion on the part of those that "own the covenant" in the New England churches; namely, that of procrastination:

> For persons merely to promise, that they will believe in Christ, or that they will hereafter comply with the conditions and duties of the covenant of grace, is not to own that covenant. Such persons don't profess now to enter into the covenant of grace with Christ, or into the relation of that covenant to Christ. All that they do at present, is only a speaking fair; they say, they will do it hereafter; . . . But what is such a profession good for, and what credit is to be given to such promises of future obedience?[39]

Such procrastination of intent coheres with the notion described by Edwards as "a giving up ourselves to him with reserve," and it lies in humanity's

35. Edwards, *Ecclesiastical Writings*, 210.
36. Edwards, *Religious Affections*, 222.
37. Edwards, *Ecclesiastical Writings*, 226.
38. Edwards, *Ecclesiastical Writings*, 206.
39. Edwards, *Ecclesiastical Writings*, 209.

innate tendency to put and keep God at a distance. Thus, if there is, on humanity's part, a spatial aspect to their putting and keeping God at a distance, there is also a temporal aspect. Such an evasion is no owning of the covenant, Edwards insists, but is, for the present at least, a visible rejection of the covenant. Moreover, such an owning of the covenant is, he contends, tantamount to the absurdity of a woman's marrying a man with the promise of "renouncing all others," not yet, but hereafter, at some point in the future. Promises of a merely future obedience to Christ in redemption are as empty and absurd as promises of a merely future fidelity in marriage. "Godliness," Edwards insists in *Religious Affections,* "consists not in an heart to intend to do the will of God, but in an heart to do it."[40]

"A SPECULATIVE FAITH"

Synonymous with Edwards's concept of "an historical faith" is his concept of "a speculative faith." In *Qualifications for Communion,* he insists upon the inadequacy of such a faith: "One end of a public profession of religion is the giving public honor to God. But surely the profession of inward esteem and a supreme respect of heart towards God is as agreeable to this design, and more directly tending to it, than the declaring of right speculative notions of him."[41] The theme of "a speculative faith," "speculative knowledge," "a speculative assent," or "right speculative notions" is a theme to which Edwards constantly returns. *True Grace Distinguished from the Faith of Devils* was a sermon preached before the Synod of New York in 1752 in the aftermath of the communion controversy; it was, unquestionably, in large part a defense and a clarification of his position in that controversy. Edwards states the following as his second inference: "We may hence infer, that no degree of speculative knowledge of things of religion, is any certain sign of saving grace."[42] The Stockbridge preacher-theologian then goes on to illustrate this truth, so pivotal to his fundamental position in the communion controversy, via the fact of the doctrinal orthodoxy of the devil:

> It may also be inferred from what has been observed, that for persons merely to yield a speculative assent to the doctrines of religion as true, is no certain evidence of a state of grace. My text tells us, that the devils "believe," and as they believe that there is one God, so they believe the truth of the doctrines of religion in general. The devil is orthodox in his faith; he believes the true

40. Edwards, *Religious Affections*, 427.
41. Edwards, *Ecclesiastical Writings*, 219.
42. Edwards, *Sermons and Discourses, 1743–1758*, 613.

> scheme of doctrine; he is no Deist, Socinian, Arian, Pelagian, or Antinomian; the articles of his faith are all sound, and what he is thoroughly established in.[43]

Edwards's concept of "a speculative faith" bears, interestingly, a twofold relationship to the concept of divine immediacy. On the one hand "a speculative faith" is, by definition, characterized by the absence of the immediate activity of God. It is this fundamental fact that, in Edwards's view, distinguishes "a speculative faith" from true, saving faith. In the latter, God acts immediately as the First Cause—a divine and supernatural light is immediately imparted to the soul by the Spirit of God. In the former, the knowledge or understanding is imparted mediately via second causes. This speculative or historical knowledge of God is in the same category as "the knowledge of human arts and sciences, and skill in temporal affairs."[44] "Flesh and blood is made use of by God as the mediate or second cause of it: he conveys it by the power and influence of natural means."[45] Moreover, the issues of immediacy and mediacy clearly reflect the relative value and importance of the gifts under consideration: "How rational is it to suppose that God, however he has left meaner goods and lower gifts to second causes, and in some sort in their power, yet should reserve this most excellent, divine, and important of all divine communications, in his own hands, to be bestowed immediately by himself, as a thing too great for second causes to be concerned in?"[46] The very fact of the immediate activity in the imparting of this divine, supernatural light is a token of the magnitude and the excellency of the gift itself. "'Tis a kind of emanation of God's beauty, and is related to God as light is to the sun."[47]

On the other hand, "a speculative faith" is itself a telling manifestation of humanity's inveterate tendency to push God away and to keep him at a distance. Indeed, this particular observation constitutes a recurring strand in Edwards's evangelistic preaching. In *Men Naturally God's Enemies*, for instance, he makes this observation:

> The natural tendency of the heart of man is to fly from God, and keep at a distance from him, as far off as possible. A natural man is averse to communion with God, and is naturally disinclined

43. Edwards, *Sermons and Discourses, 1743–1758*, 617.
44. Edwards, *Divine and Supernatural Light*, 409.
45. Edwards, *Divine and Supernatural Light*, 409.
46. Edwards, *Sermons and Discourses, 1730–1733*, 422.
47. Edwards, *Sermons and Discourses, 1730–1733*, 422.

> to those exercises of religion, wherein he has immediately to do with him.[48]

The theme of "speculative knowledge" or "speculative faith" is a theme to which Edwards returns in *Religious Affections:* "He that has doctrinal knowledge and speculation only, without affection, never is engaged in the business of religion."[49] "If the great things of religion are rightly understood, they will affect the heart."[50] The genius of "a speculative faith," from the standpoint of the religious worldling, was that it enabled him, firstly under the Halfway Covenant and then under Stoddardism, both to draw nigh and to stand afar off. Possessed of *notitia* and *assensus,* yet devoid of *fiducia,* the New Englander of the late-seventeenth century and of the early half of the eighteenth was able, by means of these two compromise systems, to enjoy "covenant favors or honors"[51] which permitted him, in turn, firstly to plant one foot in the church, and then two; yet all the while to be marked by no true submission to Christ as Savior and Lord, by no hearty compliance with the actual terms of the covenant of grace, and by no closing with Christ. "Speculative assent" or "historical faith" was thus a mechanism that was tailored to keep God and Christ at bay; it was a significant aspect of humanity's sinful counterblast to the immediacy of God in redemption. It is important to note that, while Jonathan Edwards was born into the age of deism and waged constant warfare against deism as a movement in England and France, he also appears to have been supremely convinced of what we might call the practical deism—indeed, the natural deism—of the human heart.

"MORAL SINCERITY"

Closely related to the issue of "historical faith" is the issue of "moral sincerity." Edwards deals with this vital issue early in his treatise: "The thing which must be visible and probable, in order to *visible* saintship, must be saintship *itself,* or real grace and true holiness; not visibility of saintship, not unregenerate morality, not mere moral sincerity."[52] "The visibility, that visible Christians had of saintship in the apostles' days, was not of moral sincerity, but gracious sincerity, or saving saintship."[53] Edwards sets "moral

48. Hickman, *Works of Jonathan Edwards*, 2.131.
49. Edwards, *Religious Affections*, 101.
50. Edwards, *Religious Affections*, 120.
51. Edwards, *Ecclesiastical Writings*, 316.
52. Edwards, *Ecclesiastical Writings*, 185.
53. Edwards, *Ecclesiastical Writings*, 194.

sincerity" in antithesis to "gracious sincerity" and sets the "morally sincere" in antithesis to the "evangelically sincere." He makes it clear, through his use of synonyms and synonymous phrases, that "moral sincerity" is identical with "moral seriousness," with "unregenerate morality," with "virtue, or common grace"; he clearly has in mind "those who are visibly moral livers, and only profess common virtues."[54] Moreover, in the final analysis, "moral sincerity" or "moral seriousness" must be construed as a subtle, quasi-religious manifestation of humanity's inveterate tendency towards the religion of self-justification. "'Tis inexpressible, and almost inconceivable," Edwards contends in *Religious Affections,* "how strong a self-righteous, self-exalting disposition is naturally in man."[55] "This overvaluing of common grace, and moral sincerity,"[56] as he describes it, is simply a further, extraordinary demonstration, within a New England Puritan context, of humanity's "inexpressible, and almost inconceivable" urge to reject the God-righteousness of the gospel of Christ and to embrace the human righteousness native to them. Once again, as in the issue of God's immediacy in the act of regeneration, we note the careful antithesis in Edwards's mind between the divine and the human, between the supernatural and the natural. In each sphere, whether that of the will or that of ecclesiology, the immediacy of God safeguards and guarantees the divine, supernatural, gracious character of the act or the activity in question.

With all due respect to Hall, then, it is important to note that, as the communion controversy gathered momentum in the late 1740s, the Northampton divine became increasingly convinced that there *was,* in fact, a significant connection between the Northamptonites' lax views with regard to admission to the Lord's Supper and the growth of Arminianizing views of human nature. In 1752, Edwards sent an open letter from Stockbridge to his former congregation in Northampton, appended to the end of *Misrepresentations Corrected*, his devastating response to his cousin, Solomon Williams. It is important to note that in this letter, Edwards specifically referred to "the new, fashionable, lax schemes of divinity, which have so greatly prevailed in New England of late,"[57] and he pointedly notes the affinity between the doctrinal position of his cousin, "Mr. Williams of Lebanon,"[58] and that of "Mr. Taylor, of Norwich in England."[59] Stoddardism and Arminianism

54. Edwards, *Ecclesiastical Writings*, 323.
55. Edwards, *Religious Affections*, 315.
56. Edwards, *Ecclesiastical Writings*, 317.
57. Edwards, *Ecclesiastical Writings*, 502.
58. Edwards, *Ecclesiastical Writings*, 498.
59. Edwards, *Ecclesiastical Writings*, 501–02.

were indeed, in Edwards's mind, related: lax views with regard to the Lord's Supper were symptomatic of lax views with regard to human nature.

George M. Marsden explains thus the connection between Solomon Williams's emphasis upon "moral sincerity" as the criterion for admission to the Lord's Supper and the eighteenth century's emphasis upon "virtue":

> "Virtue" was becoming the watchword of eighteenth-century thought. Modern thinkers characteristically saw virtue as a universal natural human trait that might be employed as the basis for society and cultivated as both the source and object of religion. The Northamptonites' perplexities at excluding good citizens from the church were a reflection of such trends. The theological implications of such sentiments were far larger. If modern ideas of virtue became the standards by which to judge theology, as they already were in most of the British domain, Calvinism would soon disappear.[60]

Contra Hall, we should note here, in the context of the communion controversy, not only Edwards's use of the language of "laxness," but also the correlation, in his mind, of the theological principles of Stoddardism and those of Arminianism. This issue of "moral sincerity" demonstrates once again the naturalizing, moralizing tendency of the early and mid-eighteenth century—it was simply an aspect of what Fiering describes as the benevolist and humanitarian pull of the age.[61]

For Edwards the innovations of the Halfway Covenant and Stoddardism interfered drastically with a correct understanding of the mechanism of the gospel, which is that of bringing sinners to Christ. For its part, the Halfway Covenant granted baptism almost automatically to successive generations of New Englanders and left them potentially complacent, evidently satisfied with a second-rate standing. Stoddardism, for its part, granted the Lord's Supper, potentially, to those who made no pretension to faith in Christ and yet gave them, to all intents and purposes, a first-rate standing. Paradoxically, in contrast with early New England Puritanism, these innovations did not (on the one hand) really permit the distinction between the real and the counterfeit or the application of the category of the hypocrite, and yet (on the other hand), as Edwards repeatedly insisted, their tendency was continually that of generating the counterfeit and confirming the hypocrite in his hypocrisy. Edwards was convinced that, both in theory and in practice, the innovations of the Congregational churches of New England did not and could not keep people on their mettle spiritually—indeed, that

60. Marsden, *Jonathan Edwards*, 449.

61. See Fiering, *Edwards's Moral Thought*, 200–60.

the net effect of a system that insisted only on "moral sincerity" was that of producing what he describes as "religion of a lower kind";[62] indeed, "quite another sort of saintship."[63]

THE CENTRALITY OF "THE HEART"

It is manifest from this particular controversy, and, indeed, from his entire *oeuvre*, that Edwards's supreme anthropological concern was with the heart. Indeed, Edwards insists that this is God's supreme concern: "Christ came into the world to engage in a war with God's enemies, sin and Satan; and a great war there is maintained between them; . . . and the contest is, who shall have the possession of *our hearts*."[64] The problem with a historical or speculative faith was precisely that it involved the mind, but not the heart. Such a faith involved knowledge, doctrinal understanding, orthodoxy, and assent; but it did not involve the heart or the will. Assent does not necessarily entail consent. "The consent of the will," "the consent of the heart," submission, or *fiducia* (trust or commitment)—this was the crucial element that was absent. The problem with Stoddardism was that it fostered a concept of faith that was akin to what B.B. Warfield describes as "the Romish conception which limits faith to the assent of the understanding."[65] "The stress of the Protestant definition," notes Warfield, "lies . . . upon the fiducial element."[66] Warfield goes on to comment on the well-integrated nature of true faith: "In every movement of faith, therefore, from the lowest to the highest, there is an intellectual, an emotional, and a voluntary element."[67] It was precisely this voluntary element, this fiducial element—and inevitably, perhaps, the emotional element also—that was absent from Stoddard's innovative measures.

Similarly, the problem with moral sincerity was precisely that it involved the external, but not the internal. It involved what Edwards describes as "the outside of religion,"[68] "external respect,"[69] or "external honour"[70]—but not the internal aspects of religion, not the inside of religion. What use,

62. Edwards, *Ecclesiastical Writings*, 356.
63. Edwards, *Ecclesiastical Writings*, 191.
64. Edwards, *Ecclesiastical Writings*, 220.
65. Warfield, *Works*, 340.
66. Warfield, *Works*, 340.
67. Warfield, *Works*, 341.
68. Hickman, *Works of Jonathan Edwards*, 2.72.
69. Hickman, *Works of Jonathan Edwards*, 2.136.
70. Hickman, *Works of Jonathan Edwards*, 2.136.

Edwards asks, in effect, is the head without the heart, the external without the internal, the name without the thing? What use, he asks, is the superficial, the façade, the show, the sham? He writes:

> Now why is it looked upon so dreadful, to have great numbers going without the name and honorable badge of Christianity, . . . when at the same time it is no more resented and laid to heart, that such multitudes go without the thing, which is infinitely more dreadful? Why are we so silent about this? What is the name good for, without the thing? . . . [Y]et how can parents be contented with the sign, exclusive of the thing signified! Why should they covet the external honor for their children, while they are so careless about the spiritual blessing![71]

In Edwards's view, both the Halfway Covenant and Stoddardism generated mere nominal religion—they simply generated a more respectable, quasi-Christian form of hypocrisy. His great concern was to move away from a dead, formalistic, and even hypocritical religion to a real, vital, and dynamic conception of Christianity. The great issue for Edwards was, quite simply, this: Who shall have the possession of *our hearts*?

Edwards's constant emphasis upon the heart within the context of the immediacy of God coheres with his use of the marriage metaphor:

> Owning the covenant is professing to make the transaction of that covenant our own. The transaction of that covenant is that of espousals to Christ; on our part, it is giving our souls to Christ as his spouse; there is no one thing, that the covenant of grace is so often compared to in Scripture, as the marriage-covenant; and the visible transaction, or mutual profession there is between Christ and the visible church, is abundantly compared to the mutual profession there is in marriage. In marriage the bride professes to yield to the bridegroom's suit, and to take him for her husband, renouncing all others, and to give up herself to him to be entirely and forever possessed by him as his wife. But he that professes this towards Christ, professes saving faith.[72]

The parallel established here is, of course, that between the bride being joined to the bridegroom in the covenant of marriage and the soul's closing with Christ in the covenant of grace. Edwards emphasizes at this point in his treatise that each relationship, by definition, involves not merely "the assent

71. Edwards, *Ecclesiastical Writings*, 316.

72. Edwards, *Ecclesiastical Writings*, 205.

of our understandings,"[73] but also "the consent of our hearts"[74] and "the consent of our wills."[75] The marriage relationship, Edwards argues, is not one of distance and remoteness, but one of closeness and nearness; it involves immediacy, intimacy, and union. Similarly, coming to Christ, in which "the uniting act" is "the act of faith,"[76] results in a relationship of closeness and nearness; it involves immediacy, intimacy, and union. Indeed, Edwards makes this observation: "[S]o Christ has chosen his church for a peculiar nearness to him, as his flesh and his bone."[77] The marriage metaphor is, of course, a biblical metaphor; but it is a metaphor that is pressed into service by Edwards in the cause of divine immediacy. It is important to note that, in the philosophy and the theology of Jonathan Edwards, the immediacy of God has significant soteriological and ecclesiological implications.

A CERTAIN TYPE OF PIETY

Edwards's preeminent concern in this controversy was, therefore, that of establishing a system that was conducive to a certain type of piety; namely, what he describes in his treatise as "true piety," "piety of heart," and "real vital godliness." Indeed, throughout his writings Edwards constantly idealizes a certain type of piety which he describes, variously, as "true religion," "true virtue," "true grace," "real religion," "vital religion," "vital piety," "heart religion," and "experimental religion." This is the piety of the experimental Calvinistic tradition—the kind of piety that was exemplified by little Phebe Bartlet and by the dying Abigail Hutchinson in the Northampton revival of 1734–1735; by the English evangelist, George Whitefield; by Edwards's wife, Sarah; by Edwards's uncle, William Williams; by David Brainerd, the legendary missionary to the Indians; by another uncle, Colonel John Stoddard; and (we may add) by Jonathan Edwards himself. It was this type of piety, and this alone, that was for Edwards consonant with the immediacy of God. It is important to note at this point that, although the concept of divine immediacy is basically a metaphysical concept, it is also a concept that has implications that are psychological, spiritual, and ecclesiological. Edwards is clearly moving into the hinterland at this point; he is, in effect, asking the question: What is it that coheres with this metaphysical immediacy? What secures or undergirds it? His concern here was a practical, pastoral concern:

73. Edwards, *Ecclesiastical Writings*, 205.
74. Edwards, *Ecclesiastical Writings*, 205.
75. Edwards, *Ecclesiastical Writings*, 205.
76. Edwards, *Ecclesiastical Writings*, 206.
77. Edwards, *Sermons and Discourses, 1743–1758*, 179.

it was that "Mr. Stoddard's Way"[78] was, in fact, a system that, far from promoting or securing this metaphysical immediacy, actually undermined it and issued in the externalization of religion. Edwards's supreme concern in the related controversies surrounding both the Halfway Covenant and Stoddardism was that each of these compromise systems simply fostered the externalization of religion—indeed, in the final analysis, they simply fostered the externalization of God.

NOMINAL CHRISTIANITY

One of the most common manifestations of the externalization of religion is that of a merely nominal Christianity. Edwards was clearly convinced that such a Christianity was the inevitable corollary of both the Halfway Covenant and Stoddardism. Indeed, this theme of nominal religion is a theme upon which Edwards increasingly insists as he moves towards the conclusion of *Qualifications for Communion:*

> For is it not found by constant experience through all ages, that blind corrupt mankind, in matters of religion, are strongly disposed to rest in a name instead of the thing; in the shadow, instead of the substance; and to make themselves easy with the former, in the neglect of the latter? This over-valuing of common grace, and moral sincerity, as it is called; this building so much upon them, making them the conditions of enjoying the seals of God's covenant, and the appointed privileges, and honorable and sacred badges of God's children; this, I cannot but think, naturally tends to sooth and flatter the pride of vain man, while it tends to aggrandize those things in men's eyes, which they, of themselves, are strongly disposed to magnify and trust in.[79]

If the Halfway Covenant gave New Englanders one badge of Christianity, Stoddardism gave them two. But the problem as far as Edwards was concerned was that, by embracing these expedients, these compromise systems, New Englanders were resting in the name rather than the thing, in the shadow rather than the substance, in the badge rather than the reality. "And in truth," Edwards insists, "it is no honor at all to a man, to have merely the outward badges of a Christian, without being a Christian indeed."[80] "What

78. Cited in Edwards, *Ecclesiastical Writings*, 19.

79. Edwards, *Ecclesiastical Writings*, 317.

80. Edwards, *Ecclesiastical Writings*, 316.

is the name good for," asks Edwards incisively, "without the thing?"[81] The evangelical sacramentalism that had, astonishingly, developed in New England over the course of the previous one-hundred years had, in Edwards's view, simply tended to generate several generations of merely nominal Christians.

Inextricably connected with the issue of nominal religion is the issue of hypocrisy. Hypocrisy, or the cult of the mask, is one of the greatest expressions of the externalization of religion; it is the religion of the façade. In *Religious Affections* (1746) Edwards posits "two sorts of hypocrites"—indeed, he cites with approval Thomas Shepard's distinction between "legal hypocrites" on the one hand and "evangelical hypocrites" on the other:

> There are two sorts of hypocrites: one that are deceived with their outward morality and external religion; many of which are professed Arminians, in the doctrine of justification: and the other, are those that are deceived with false discoveries and elevations.[82]

By "evangelical hypocrites," Edwards clearly intends "such as are deceived with false discoveries and elevations"; this type of hypocrite was particularly prominent at the time of the Great Awakening. By "legal hypocrites," Edwards clearly intends "such as are deceived with their own outward morality and external religion; many of whom are professed Arminians, in the doctrine of justification"; this type of hypocrite, while potentially present in the church at all times, became increasingly prominent in the latter half of the 1740s as the Great Awakening receded and as the Communion Controversy gathered momentum. The very concept of "moral sincerity" or "moral seriousness," so integral to Stoddardism, simply demonstrates the subtly externalizing, Arminianizing tendency of that system. In more general vein, Edwards makes this observation: "There are multitudes of men that wear the guise of saints, appear like saints, and their state, both in their own eyes and in the eyes of their neighbours, is good. They have sheep's clothing."[83] Thus the legal hypocrite dons the mask of externalities, not least that of the two sacraments, and supposes that "all these external performances" will suffice before the Judge of all the earth. As Christ amply demonstrates in the Gospels, such hypocrisy is inevitable to some extent in the kingdom of heaven; the problem in Edwards's mind is that this species of hypocrisy is inevitably exacerbated and actually promoted both by the Halfway Covenant

81. Edwards, *Ecclesiastical Writings*, 316.

82. Edwards, *Religious Affections*, 173.

83. Hickman, *Works of Jonathan Edwards*, 2.200.

and by Stoddardism. Both systems simply encourage the inclusion of those that he describes as "gospel-sinners and domestic enemies in the house of God."[84]

THE EXTERNALIZATION OF RELIGION

It is important to note at this juncture that Edwards did not deny that there is an external aspect to the covenant of grace:

> I know the distinction that is made by some, between the internal and external covenant; but I hope, the divines that make this distinction, would not be understood, that there are really and properly two covenants of grace; but only that those who profess the one only covenant of grace, are of two sorts; there are those who comply with it internally and really, and others who do so only externally, that is, in profession and visibility. But he that externally and visibly complies with the covenant of grace, appears and professes to do so really.[85]

The distinction to which Edwards refers here is, of course, a classic tenet of Reformed theology—it is the distinction between being *in foedere* (in the covenant) or *de foedere* (of the covenant). The children of believers are, by definition, *in foedere;* they are, necessarily, *in* the covenant in an external sense and enjoy its external blessings and privileges. They are not, by definition, *de foedere;* they are not, necessarily, *of* the covenant in an internal sense or marked by a hearty compliance with its terms. Thus it is possible for a child of the covenant to belong to the covenant in an external sense, but, on account of the absence of repentance and faith, not to belong to the covenant in an internal sense. Classically, in Reformed circles such a child would, of course, be deemed to be a candidate for baptism, but not a candidate for the Lord's Supper. By permitting such a child or young person to partake of the Lord's Supper, therefore, Stoddardism effectively denied this crucial distinction and extended to those who belong only in an external sense the rights and privileges proper to those who belong in an internal sense. The net effect of this, in Edwards's mind, is that the church actually condones and endorses a show and a sham; in the name of a *prima facie* internalization of religion it actually condones and endorses a *de facto* externalization of God.

84. Edwards, *Ecclesiastical Writings*, 255.

85. Edwards, *Ecclesiastical Writings*, 206.

Classically, in the Reformed tradition, Roman Catholicism is regarded as the supreme example of the externalization of religion. The great emphasis upon the visible church, the sacramental principle, the *ex opere operato* concept (out of the work worked; i.e., automatically), the doctrine of baptismal regeneration, the whole notion of sacramental grace—it is this sacramental system that, above all else, results in the externalization of Christianity. After all, in the Reformed tradition the sacraments are construed as outward and visible signs of inward and spiritual grace. These outward, visible signs do not mediate saving grace *ab extra* (from outside); they signify saving grace in the soul. Indeed, they presuppose the existence of that grace. It should be noted, therefore, that there is a very significant connection between an over-emphasis upon the sacraments (be it of the efficacy of the sacraments, as in Roman Catholicism, or of the availability of the sacraments, as in Stoddardism) and the externalization of religion. Solomon Stoddard was, of course, no Roman Catholic, and Stoddardism was not Roman Catholicism. Nevertheless, there is, surely, inherent within Stoddard's inconsistent system a kind of evangelical externalization of religion precisely because of his evident willingness to make both outward signs available to those who, on his own avowed principles, do not possess the inward grace they signify. The inherent tendency of both the Halfway Covenant and Stoddardism was always that of drifting irresistibly in the direction of the great Romanist principle, *Ubi ecclesia, ibi Spiritus* (Where the church is, there the Spirit is)—a quasi-Romanist conception of faith tends inevitably in the direction of a quasi-Romanist conception of the church. Edwards's insistence was always upon the great Protestant counterblast to that principle: *Ubi Spiritus, ibi ecclesia* (Where the Spirit is, there the church is).

IMMEDIACY IN RELATION TO GOD

Geoffrey F. Nuttall has, interestingly, described the Puritan movement as "a movement towards immediacy in relation to God."[86] The Puritan mind was convinced that it was not only the Church of Rome that put and kept God at a distance, but also, in a measure, the Church of England. The Puritan experiment in the New World in the 1630s and 1640s had been an attempt to restore both the concept and the practice of divine immediacy to the soul's relationship with God, and ecclesiology lay at the very heart of this attempt. "Mr. Stoddard's way" was, however, as far as his grandson was concerned, a *de facto* reversal of the "New England experiment." The Halfway Covenant and Stoddardism clearly involved a much more relaxed, inclusive, and

86. Nuttall, *Holy Spirit*, 134.

comprehensive view of the church and fostered what Morgan describes as "a more worldly purity."[87] Edwards's response to "the silent revolution" triggered by these successive compromise systems was to launch a revolution of his own—a revolution rooted and grounded once again in the concept of ecclesiastical purity. Thus if, as Edwards believed, his ecclesiology was such that it designedly produced churches that might be described as "so close to God and so far from the world,"[88] the ecclesiology introduced by his grandfather was such that it produced churches that might be described (at least in part) as "so close to the world and so far from God." Just as there was a crucial connection in Edwards's mind between the concepts of inclusiveness, worldliness, externalization, and distance, so there was also a crucial connection in his mind between the concepts of exclusiveness, purity, internalization, and immediacy. There can be no doubt but that the issue of "immediacy in relation to God" lay at the very heart of the distinctly Puritan ecclesiology reintroduced by Jonathan Edwards into the ecclesiastical world of mid-eighteenth-century New England.

87. Morgan, *Visible Saints*, 150.

88. Morgan, *Visible Saints*, 114.

SPIRITUAL EXPERIENCE

"ENTHUSIASM"

"'Enthusiasm' in the religious sense," observes Ronald A. Knox in his classic study, *Enthusiasm: A Chapter in the History of Religion* (1950), "belongs to the seventeenth and eighteenth centuries."[1] "For a hundred and fifty years, it becomes the major preoccupation of religious minds . . . The Quakers are first in the field."[2] The one hundred and fifty years under consideration run approximately from the year 1650 unto the end of the eighteenth century. It is part of the fascination of the life and the ministry of Jonathan Edwards (1703–1758) that he was born into a transatlantic intellectual and religious world in which, *inter alia,* the issue of "enthusiasm" was of great contemporary relevance, and it presented him with a battle that had to be fought on two fronts, for the world into which Edwards was born was not merely the world of Quakerism—it was also, in the course of his own lifetime, the world of the Great Awakening in America and of the Evangelical Revival in England; indeed, Edwards was the most influential American preacher-theologian in the Great Awakening (1740–1742).[3] The inveterate opponent of "enthusiasm," Edwards was himself, paradoxically, regarded by some as

1. Knox, *Enthusiasm*, 6.

2. Knox, *Enthusiasm*, 4.

3. With regard to the respective abilities and influence of Jonathan Edwards and George Whitefield, there is no doubt in my mind that Whitefield was the greater and more influential preacher of the two; just as there is no doubt in my mind that Edwards was the greater and more influential theologian of the two.

the friend of "enthusiasm" in what he himself describes, not without irony, as "that enthusiastical town of Northampton."[4]

This very fact demonstrates the elusiveness of the concept of "enthusiasm"—"enthusiasm" tends often to be a matter of perspective. Indeed, it might well be said that "enthusiasm" is, at least to some extent, in the eye of the beholder. "The historical phenomenon of enthusiasm in the seventeenth and eighteenth centuries," observes Michael Heyd, "is therefore primarily a phenomenon of the reaction to enthusiasm, shedding light above all on the changing religious sensibilities of its critics. Nevertheless some recurrent characteristics of 'enthusiasm' may be identified."[5] Heyd goes on, significantly, to identify "an element of immediacy, lack of distance, and intuition in . . . the experience of the enthusiast."[6] It is evident that the issue of the immediacy of God, indeed, the issue of the immediacy of the soul's approach to God, lies at the very center of the controversy that swirls around the elusive and certainly pejorative concept of "enthusiasm."

More precisely, Knox defines "enthusiasm" as "ultra-supernaturalism." "If I could have been certain of the reader's goodwill," he admits somewhat tentatively, "I would have called my tendency 'ultra-supernaturalism.' For that is the real character of the enthusiast."[7] The idea here is, clearly, that of an excessive, exaggerated, and spurious supernaturalism. Knox's definition is, we believe, incisive; but there remains the fundamental problem of perspective. As a Roman Catholic, Knox regarded the evangelical doctrine of the "new birth" as "enthusiastic." By this yardstick, Jonathan Edwards himself, not to mention George Whitefield, would, of course, have been regarded as enthusiasts. From Edwards's perspective, however, the doctrine of the new birth was central to the scriptural, evangelical, and reformed system that he had embraced, and the immediacy of God was central to the doctrine of the new birth. Edwards's own battle against "enthusiasm" or "ultra-supernaturalism" was, therefore, a battle against what we might call ultra-immediacy—for Edwards there was a true immediacy and there was a false immediacy, and a false immediacy is, in the final analysis, no immediacy at all.

4. Edwards, *Great Awakening*, 334.

5. *Encyclopedia of the Enlightenment*, s.v. "enthusiasm."

6. *Encyclopedia of the Enlightenment*, s.v. "enthusiasm."

7. Knox, *Enthusiasm*, 2.

QUAKERISM

Edwards's opposition to this spurious, illegitimate immediacy is demonstrated by his inveterate anti-Quakerism. Originating with and flowering under George Fox (1624–1691) in England from 1652 onwards, the Quaker movement had developed significantly on the other side of the Atlantic in Rhode Island, Massachusetts, and Pennsylvania in the third and, especially, the fourth quarter of the seventeenth century. Jonathan Edwards was thus born into a world in which Quakerism was very much a crucial, albeit unorthodox, element in the religious spirit of the age. The most significant feature of this movement was, surely, the doctrine of "the inner light" or "the light within." Thus, although there is, in the earlier phases of the Quaker movement, evidence of some commitment to the Scriptures as the Word of God, the constant drift of the movement was away from the concept of external, objective revelation and towards the concept of internal, subjective revelation—a revelation that was, supposedly, immediate. Knox specifically mentions, interestingly, the Quaker dislike of "a religion which was all at a distance, grounded on the report of Christ dying at Jerusalem."[8] The emphasis of the Quakers was upon the directness of God's communications, upon *hearing Christ* rather than *hearing of Christ,* and upon the notion that "Christ has come to teach His people Himself." There was, in the Quaker mind, an increasing diffidence with regard to the historical objectivities of the Christian faith and a corresponding gravitation towards its more subjective aspects. "What is most distinctive of the Society," notes *The New Schaff-Herzog Encyclopedia of Religious Knowledge,* "is its belief in the immediate influence of the Holy Spirit, and its expectation of the guidance of the Spirit in worship and all religious acts."[9] Geoffrey F. Nuttall, for his part, notes in Quakerism a claim to "an immediate consciousness" and to "immediate leadings by the Holy Spirit in the sphere of practical activity."[10] It is evident, then, that the concept of divine immediacy was pivotal to the Quaker *Weltanschauung;* it is also evident that this particular species of divine immediacy was, as far as Edwards was concerned, an illegitimate immediacy. Edwards emphasizes that the Spirit of God does not testify to "any mystical, fantastical Christ; such as the light within, which the spirit of the Quakers

8. Cited in Knox, *Enthusiasm*, 153.

9. *New Schaff-Herzog Encyclopedia*, s.v. "Friends, Society of."

10. Nuttall, *Holy Spirit*, 53.

extols."[11] In 1671, just three decades before Edwards's birth, Quakerism had been described as "the fag-end of the Reformation."[12]

IMPRUDENCES IN THE GREAT AWAKENING

It is crucial to note, however, that Quaker-like tendencies were manifested by many non-Quakers at the time of the Great Awakening. "Many godly persons," notes Edwards in *The Distinguishing Marks of a Work of the Spirit of God* (1741), "have undoubtedly in this and other ages, exposed themselves to woeful delusions, by an aptness to lay too much weight on impulses and impressions, as if they were immediate revelations from God, to signify something future, or to direct them where to go and what to do."[13] In *Religious Affections* (1746), Edwards develops his analysis of this tendency in terms of "a kind of conversation" that is carried on between God and them:

> They have often particular words of Scripture, sweet declarations and promises suggested to 'em, which by reason of the manner of their coming, they think are immediately sent from God to them, at that time; which they look upon as their warrant to take 'em; and which they actually make the main ground of their appropriating them to themselves, and of the comfort they take in them, and the confidence they receive from them. Thus they imagine a kind of conversation is carried on between God and them; and that God, from time to time, does, as it were, immediately speak to 'em, and satisfy their doubts and testifies his love to 'em, and promises 'em supports and supplies, and his blessing in such and such cases, and reveals to 'em clearly their interest in eternal blessings. And thus they are often elevated, and have a course of a sudden and tumultuous kind of joys, mingled with a strong confidence, and high opinion of themselves; when indeed the main ground of these joys, and this confidence is not anything contained in, or taught by these Scriptures, as they lie in the Bible, but the manner of their coming to them; which is a certain evidence of their delusion.[14]

We have already noted, in the context of ecclesiology, that in *Religious Affections* (1746), Edwards postulates "two sorts of hypocrites"—not only those that are "deceived with their outward morality and external religion,"

11. Edwards, *Great Awakening*, 250.
12. Cited in Nuttall, *Holy Spirit*, 13.
13. Edwards, *Great Awakening*, 244.
14. Edwards, *Religious Affections*, 223–24.

but also those that are "deceived with false discoveries and elevations."[15] Edwards notes that the latter—these "evangelical hypocrites," as he terms them—are characterized by "impulses and supposed revelations,"[16] by "impulses and imagined revelations."[17] In Edwards's mind, one of the great dangers of this ultra-supernaturalism was that those who supposedly experience this divine immediacy place their confidence in the very fact of it—that is to say, place their confidence in the manner in which (for instance) words of Scripture come to mind. Edwards makes at this juncture a crucial distinction between the manner of the experience and the nature of the experience. To build upon the former rather than upon the latter, Edwards insists, is to build upon a precarious foundation—to build, in effect, upon this ultra-immediacy is to build upon "a false and sandy foundation for faith."[18]

In *Some Thoughts Concerning the Revival* (1743), Edwards demonstrates further the danger and the gravity of this notion of "immediate revelation"[19] or "immediate direction from heaven"[20]:

> And one erroneous principle, than which scarce any has proved more mischievous to the present glorious work of God, is a notion that 'tis God's manner now in these days to guide his saints . . . by inspiration, or immediate revelation; and to make known to 'em what shall come to pass hereafter, or what it is his will that they should do, by impressions that he by his Spirit makes upon their minds, either with or without texts of Scripture; whereby something is made known to them, that is not taught in the Scripture as the words lie in the Bible.[21]

"This error," Edwards continues, "will defend and support errors. As long as a person has a notion that he is guided by immediate direction from heaven, it makes him incorrigible and impregnable in all his misconduct."[22] It is important to note that Edwards is consistently unsparing in his critique of the spurious ultra-immediacy which forsakes the light of external, objective revelation in favor of internal, subjective inspiration. The net effect of this "one erroneous principle," Edwards insists, is "soon to bring the

15. Edwards, *Religious Affections*, 173.
16. Edwards, *Religious Affections*, 173.
17. Edwards, *Religious Affections*, 173.
18. Edwards, *Religious Affections*, 223.
19. Edwards, *Great Awakening*, 432.
20. Edwards, *Great Awakening*, 432.
21. Edwards, *Great Awakening*, 432.
22. Edwards, *Great Awakening*, 432.

Bible into neglect and contempt."[23] This, he contends in *The Distinguishing Marks*, is, in effect, to "leave the guidance of the pole star to follow a Jack-with-a-lanthorn."[24]

ULTRA-IMMEDIACY

"This bastard religion,"[25] as Edwards unflinchingly describes this phenomenon in *Religious Affections*, consisted, then, essentially of whispers, suggestions, impulses, impressions, illuminations, external representations, immediate significations from heaven, supposed prophetical revelations, and fancied inspiration. "Many have a false notion of communion with God, as though it were carried on by impulses, and whispers, and external representations, immediately made to their imagination."[26] "They look upon these as spiritual discoveries; which is a gross delusion."[27] It is evident from *Some Thoughts Concerning the Revival* (1743) that Edwards regarded this kind of religion as constituting "superstition" and "enthusiasm."[28] *The Oxford Dictionary of the Christian Church* emphasizes that, while the original meaning of the term "enthusiasm" denotes the state of "being possessed by a god," it later assumed "the sense of fancied inspiration" or "a vain confidence of Divine favour or communication."[29] *The Oxford English Dictionary* confirms this notion of "enthusiasm" as involving "fancied inspiration," "supernatural inspiration," and claims to "special revelations" or "special divine communications." We note once again that, for Jonathan Edwards, this "ultra-supernaturalism" was rooted and grounded in an exaggerated concept of divine immediacy in the realm of spiritual experience.

EXTERNALITY

What, then, for Edwards is the hallmark of this false ultra-immediacy? What is it that distinguishes this ultra-immediacy from those "spiritual

23. Edwards, *Great Awakening*, 432.

24. Edwards, *Great Awakening*, 282. A "lanthorn" is an old British term for a "lantern."

25. Edwards, *Religious Affections*, 287.

26. Edwards, *Great Awakening*, 246.

27. Edwards, *Great Awakening*, 229.

28. In this treatise, Edwards refers to "those three extremes of enthusiasm, superstition, and severity towards opposers." Edwards, *Great Awakening*, 410.

29. *Oxford Dictionary of the Christian Church*, s.v. "enthusiasm."

discoveries" or "divine discoveries" which Edwards so strongly endorses? The answer lies in the essential externality of "false discoveries":

> Many who have had such things have very ignorantly supposed them to be of the nature of spiritual discoveries. They have had lively ideas of some external shape, and beautiful form of countenance; and this they call spiritually seeing Christ. Some have had impressed upon them ideas of a great outward light; and this they call a spiritual discovery of God's or Christ's glory. Some have had ideas of Christ's hanging on the cross, and his blood running from his wounds; and this they call a spiritual sight of Christ crucified, and the way of salvation by his blood. Some have seen him with his arms open ready to embrace them; and this they call a discovery of the sufficiency of Christ's grace and love. Some have had lively ideas of heaven, and of Christ on his throne there, and shining ranks of saints and angels; and this they call seeing heaven opened to them. Some from time to time have had a lively idea of a person of a beautiful countenance smiling upon them; and this they call a spiritual discovery of the love of Christ to their souls, and tasting the love of Christ. And they look upon it as sufficient evidence that these things are spiritual discoveries, and that they see them spiritually, because they say they don't see these things with their bodily eyes, but in their hearts; for they can see them when their eyes are shut. And in like manner, the imaginations of some have been impressed with ideas of the sense of hearing; they have had ideas of words, as if they were spoke to them, sometimes they are the words of Scripture, and sometimes other words: they have had ideas of Christ's speaking comfortable words to them. These things they have called having the inward call of Christ, hearing the voice of Christ spiritually in their hearts, having the witness of the Spirit, and the inward testimony of the love of Christ, etc.[30]

It will be noted that the focus of Edwards's critique here falls upon the external, the visible, the audible, the imaginary. Indeed, he emphasizes in this context that there is, intrinsically, nothing in the nature of these experiences that rises above "our animal senses, which senses the beasts have in as great perfection as we."[31] In the ensuing passage, Edwards emphasizes the essentially external character of false discoveries by means of the *leitmotiv* of "external ideas."[32] By "external ideas" and "outward representations,"

30. Edwards, *Religious Affections*, 211–12.

31. Edwards, *Religious Affections*, 213.

32. See Edwards, *Religious Affections*, 215.

Edwards clearly intends not only those things that are seen with the bodily eyes, but also "impressions on the imagination." For although, at first glance, "impressions upon the imagination" might be deemed to be internal, not external, Edwards argues that they are, in fact, external, not internal, precisely because they are not located in the heart. The ideas under consideration might well be internal to the mind, but they are still external to the heart. "This," Edwards contends, "is a low, miserable notion of spiritual sense."[33]

We note at this point an interesting parallel between Edwards's emphases in spiritual experience and his emphases in ecclesiology. There is, in the realm of ecclesiology, a crucial antithesis between (on the one hand) the assent of the mind, externalization, and distance, and (on the other hand) the consent of the heart, internalization, and immediacy; similarly, there is, in the realm of spiritual experience, a crucial antithesis between (on the one hand) the imagination, externality, and distance, and (on the other hand) "the sense of the heart," internality, and immediacy. The great problem with the "external ideas" found in what he calls the "evangelical hypocrite" is that there is nothing spiritual, supernatural, or divine about them. It is thus that the "evangelical hypocrite," for all his vaunted experiences, puts God at a distance and keeps God at arm's length. In the final analysis "external ideas" or "imaginary ideas" simply cohere, once again, with the externalization of religion and the externalization of God.

THE EXAMPLE OF BALAAM

The example that is most frequently adduced by Edwards in order to demonstrate the fact that the Spirit of God can and does operate as an external, extrinsic agent upon an unregenerate person is that of Balaam in the Old Testament. Edwards's purpose in his reiterated adduction of the example of Balaam is that of demonstrating that the common influences of the Spirit of God upon a person (even to the extent of the gift of prophecy) are perfectly compatible with an unregenerate state. It is a remarkable fact that, as the Scriptures demonstrate, Balaam was the recipient, indeed, the channel, of a very significant Messianic prophecy: "There shall come a Star out of Jacob, and a Scepter shall rise out of Israel" (Num 24:17). Edwards's position with regard to Balaam is that, although he was the subject of an extrinsic operation of the Spirit of God upon his mind, he was not the subject of an intrinsic operation of the Spirit upon his heart: "Thus there was no spiritual light in Balaam; though he had the will of God immediately suggested to

33. Edwards, *Religious Affections*, 213.

him by the Spirit of God from time to time."[34] "But yet had no manner of spiritual discovery of Christ; that day-star never spiritually rose in his heart, he being but a natural man."[35]

It is in this very context that Edwards lays down the crucial principle that it is grace, not gifts, or even experiences of the Spirit of God, that constitutes the crucial mark of the regeneration of the sinner: "A man may have ten thousand such revelations and directions from the Spirit of God, and yet not have a jot of grace in his heart."[36] Indeed, in this context he emphasizes that not only Balaam, but also King Saul and Judas—all of them unregenerate men as far as Edwards was concerned—were recipients of "such revelations and directions from the Spirit of God."[37] How, then, is this paradox to be explained? "'Tis of the nature of a common influence of the Spirit,"[38] Edwards insists. "'Tis no more than the gift of prophecy."[39] In a manner that is reminiscent of the teaching of the Apostle Paul in First Corinthians 13, and of his own treatment of this chapter in *Charity and its Fruits,* Edwards proceeds to lay down another crucial principle: "There is a more excellent way that the Spirit of God leads the sons of God, that natural men cannot have,"[40] namely, that of walking in the will of God, in the path of truth, and in Christian holiness, and possessing a relish and taste for spiritual things. This leading of the Spirit of God does not lie in "impressions and immediate revelations"[41] or in giving humanity "new statutes and new precepts"[42]—such things may be performed with "a cold dead heart."[43] The leading of the Spirit, of which the New Testament speaks, is a leading into God's statutes and precepts. "Christian practice," Edwards insists, "is the sign of signs."[44]

"THE SENSE OF THE HEART"

It is important to note, however, that Edwards's emphasis does not merely fall upon the practical evidence of regeneration—it also falls, and falls

34. Edwards, *Religious Affections*, 279
35. Edwards, *Religious Affections*, 215.
36. Edwards, *Great Awakening*, 436.
37. Edwards, *Great Awakening*, 436.
38. Edwards, *Great Awakening*, 436.
39. Edwards, *Great Awakening*, 436.
40. Edwards, *Great Awakening*, 436.
41. Edwards, *Great Awakening*, 438.
42. Edwards, *Great Awakening*, 437.
43. Edwards, *Great Awakening*, 437.
44. Edwards, *Religious Affections*, 444.

heavily, upon the "sensible" or "affective" evidence of regeneration. In *Religious Affections* and elsewhere throughout his *oeuvre,* Edwards lays great emphasis upon what he terms "the sense of the heart." This he describes, variously, as "a new sense," "a cordial sense," "a spiritual sense," and "that supernatural sense." These phrases are clearly synonymous, interchangeable terms. It should be noted, moreover, that the *locus* of this new, cordial, supernatural, spiritual sense is not the mind, but the heart. There is, of course, no antithesis here, on Edwards's part, between the heart and the mind—"the Sage of Northampton,"[45] as Harry S. Stout describes him, was marked by no obscurantist anti-intellectualism, here or elsewhere. Edwards's very powerful emphasis upon the mind, both in principle and in practice, is balanced by a very powerful emphasis upon the heart. Thus his emphasis falls upon the insufficiency of the mind, considered in isolation, in the sphere of divine and spiritual things. The mind is, in and of itself, sufficient for notional or speculative knowledge; the mind is not, in and of itself, sufficient for saving or gracious knowledge. It is "the sense of the heart" that, for Edwards, constitutes the crucial, distinguishing element in these two distinct types of knowledge; it thus constitutes for Edwards the defining *sine qua non* of the regenerating influences of the Spirit of God.

The following passage in *Religious Affections* is, surely, Edwards's clearest exposition of this pivotal concept of "the sense of the heart":

> From what has been said, therefore, we come necessarily to this conclusion, concerning that wherein spiritual understanding consists; viz. that it consists in a sense of the heart, of the supreme beauty and sweetness of the holiness or moral perfection of divine things, together with all that discerning and knowledge of things of religion, that depends upon, and flows from such a sense.
>
> Spiritual understanding consists primarily in a sense of heart of that spiritual beauty. I say, a sense of heart; for it is not speculation merely that is concerned in this kind of understanding; nor can there be a clear distinction made between the two faculties of understanding and will, as acting distinctly and separately, in this matter. When the mind is sensible of the sweet beauty and amiableness of a thing, that implies a sensibleness of sweetness and delight in the presence of the idea of it; and this sensibleness of the amiableness or delightfulness of beauty, carries in the very nature of it, the sense of the heart; or an effect

45. Edwards, *Sermons and Discourses, 1739–1742,* 26.

> and impression the soul is the subject of, as a substance possessed of taste, inclination and will.[46]

In *Religious Affections*, Edwards emphasizes that "this new spiritual sense" in the regenerate person is not to be construed as involving a difference in degree, but as involving a fundamental difference in kind. It is something entirely new, something that is "entirely above nature,"[47] something that is supernatural, something that originates with the Spirit of God:

> From these things it is evident, that those gracious influences which the saints are subjects of, and the effects of God's Spirit which they experience, are entirely above nature, and altogether of a different kind from anything that men find within themselves by nature, or only in the exercise of natural principles; and are things which no improvement of those qualifications, or principles that are natural, no advancing or exalting of them to higher degrees, and no kind of composition of them, will ever bring men to; because they not only differ from what is natural, and from everything that natural men experience, in degree and circumstances, but also in kind; and are of a nature vastly more excellent. And this is what I mean by supernatural, when I say, that gracious affections are from those influences that are supernatural.[48]

"A SIXTH SENSE"

Edwards's concept of "the sense of the heart" has been described by David J. Lyttle as "a sixth sense." Lyttle summarizes this aspect of Edwards's thought thus: "There is, as it were, a sixth sense, a supernatural sense, with which the saint has experiences which are radically different from natural sense experience."[49] This "spiritual or sixth sense . . . is an innate, non-cognitive principle of perception."[50] Lyttle describes this sense as "fundamentally a Calvinistic concept."[51] Moreover, a crucial part of the significance of the concept of Edwards's "sixth sense" lies in the fact that, as with the other five senses, what is experienced, and thus known, is not the result of some

46. Edwards, *Religious Affections*, 272.
47. Edwards, *Religious Affections*, 205.
48. Edwards, *Religious Affections*, 205.
49. Lyttle, "Sixth Sense," 56.
50. Lyttle, "Sixth Sense," 58.
51. Lyttle, "Sixth Sense," 50.

circuitous process of ratiocination, but is experienced, and thus known, immediately. Sense experience is always relatively immediate.[52] When the eye sees, it sees immediately; when the ear hears, it hears immediately; when the nose smells, it smells immediately; when the hand touches, it touches immediately; and when the tongue tastes, it tastes immediately. In *Religious Affections,* Edwards highlights in particular the senses of sight, hearing, and taste. He points out that the perception of the loveliness of "a beautiful countenance," or the beauty of "true harmony," or the attractiveness of "good food" is not something that requires many hours "of the most accurate reasonings," but occurs "at once," "spontaneously," "in a moment." The contrast which Edwards draws here is that between "taste" on the one hand and "judgment" on the other: whereas "the judgment" fetches "a kind of circuit," "the taste" forms its views immediately. The emphasis falls here upon the temporal aspect of immediacy; yet this temporal aspect of immediacy is, once again, inextricably connected with the causal aspect of immediacy. Indeed, it is precisely because this perception is non-inferential that it is non-sequential. Similarly, when the soul perceives the beauty and the glory of Christ in the gospel, it perceives immediately. There is, as with the other five senses, yet even more strikingly, a fundamental immediacy about Edwards's "sixth sense."

What, then, is Edwards's great concern in his concept of "the sense of the heart"? His concern is, once again, that of emphasizing and safeguarding the immediate, divine, and supernatural character of true spiritual experience. "Edwards is at pains," observes Helm, "to give a sensationalist account of spiritual experience."[53] "This is Edwards's Locke-inspired way of expressing Puritan experimental theology. Thus Edwards speaks of 'the saving influences of the Spirit of God' in terms of *sensation* and *the perception of a new simple idea*."[54] One of the fundamental tenets of Edwards's Calvinistic theology is that the unregenerate person lacks such a God-given spiritual sense. "Spiritual understanding," Helm insists, "does not consist in the possession of any new doctrinal knowledge."[55] Such doctrinal knowledge can be acquired gradually by the unregenerate person via the use of means; but "the new sense," "the sense of the heart," "the new simple idea" is given immediately by God to those he regenerates. Edwards emphasizes

52. Elwood observes that "the Puritan writers frequently employed the analogy of the immediacy of sense perception as well as that of aesthetic appreciation in describing the phenomenon of conversion." Elwood, *Philosophical Theology*, 121.

53. Helm, "Locke and Edwards," 56.

54. Helm, "Locke and Edwards," 55.

55. Helm, "Locke and Edwards," 60.

that "the new sense is qualitatively different from the other five."[56] It is, Helm contends, "the non-natural character of a truly spiritual experience"[57] that is emphasized by Edwards. "It is hard to see," Helm continues, "how Edwards could have put any more clearly his belief that spiritual experience was supernatural."[58] Thus a true religious experience involved the acquisition of another sense, a supernatural sense, what Helm describes as "the God-given sixth sense."[59]

There is, therefore, a crucial connection in Edwards's mind between "the sense of the heart, the sense of taste, and the immediacy of God." It is interesting to note that in *Religious Affections* Edwards cites Chambers' *Cyclopaedia* [*sic*] on the theme of "taste":

> The judgment forms its opinions from reflection: the reason on this occasion fetches a kind of circuit, to arrive at its end; it supposes principles, it draws consequences, and it judges; but not without a thorough knowledge of the case; . . . Good taste observes none of these formalities; e'er it has time to consult, it has taken its side; as soon as ever the object is presented it, the impression is made, the sentiment formed, ask no more of it. As the ear is wounded with a harsh sound, as the smell is soothed with an agreeable odour, before ever the reason have meddled with those objects to judge of them, so the taste opens itself at once, and prevents all reflection.[60]

The crucial point upon which Edwards insists here is that there is something non-reflective, non-inferential—something direct, intuitive, and immediate—about "the sense of the heart."

It is further evident that "the sense of the heart" involves a sense of beauty; the aesthetic element is inseparably connected with this sense. In the above passage, Edwards emphasizes the related concepts of "beauty," "sweetness," "amiableness," and "delight." The grace of God in the gospel of Christ is, he insists, not merely a "*bonum utile*"[61] ("a profitable good"); it is also a "*bonum formosum*"[62] ("a beautiful good"). Edwards defines this

56. Helm, "Locke and Edwards," 57.

57. Helm, "Locke and Edwards," 56.

58. Helm, "Locke and Edwards" 56.

59. Helm, "Locke and Edwards," 59.

60. Cited in Edwards, *Religious Affections*, 282. Chambers's *Cyclopaedia*: or, *An Universal Dictionary of Arts and Sciences* was published in London by Ephraim Chambers in 1728. This work should not be confused with Chambers's *Encyclopedia*, which was published in the following century in 1859.

61. Edwards, *Religious Affections*, 262.

62. Edwards, *Religious Affections*, 262.

"*bonum formosum*" as involving a sense of "the moral beauty of God," or a sense of "the beauty of his moral perfections." "This is the beauty of the Godhead, and the divinity of Divinity, . . . the good of the infinite Fountain of Good."[63] At the very center of Edwards's doctrine of regeneration there lies a very striking and very powerful spiritual aesthetic, the central focus of which is unquestionably the person and work of Christ.

Moreover, Edwards proceeds to emphasize a crucial distinction at this point—a distinction between this "sensible knowledge" on the one hand and "speculative knowledge" on the other:

> There is a distinction to be made between a mere notional understanding, wherein the mind only beholds things in the exercise of a speculative faculty; and the sense of the heart, wherein the mind don't only speculate and behold, but relishes and feels. That sort of knowledge, by which a man has a sensible perception of amiableness and loathsomeness, or of sweetness and nauseousness, is not just the same sort of knowledge with that, by which he knows what a triangle is, and what a square is. The one is mere speculative knowledge; the other sensible knowledge, in which more than the mere intellect is concerned; the heart is the proper subject of it, or the soul as a being that not only beholds, but has inclination, and is pleased or displeased. And yet there is the nature of instruction in it; as he that has perceived the sweet taste of honey, knows much more about it, than he who has only looked upon and felt of it.[64]

The crucial distinction upon which Edwards insists here (and, indeed, throughout his *oeuvre*) is that between (on the one hand) a notional, speculative knowledge such as knowing "what a triangle or square is," and (on the other hand) a "sensible," "affective" knowledge such as perceiving "the sweet taste of honey." By parity of reasoning, Edwards contends, it is one thing to have a merely notional opinion that "Jesus is the Christ, the Son of the living God"; it is another thing to have a "sense of the excellency of Christ." The latter position involves "the sense of the heart, wherein the mind not only speculates and beholds, but relishes and feels." "The new sense" and "the sense of the heart" found in the true believer involves, as far as Edwards is concerned, a distinct spiritual *goût* (taste); indeed, it involves a certain spiritual *gusto*. This concept of taste or relish is integral to Edwards's "cordial sense."

63. Edwards, *Religious Affections*, 274.

64. Edwards, *Religious Affections*, 272.

"THE VEIL"

"The sense of the heart" is also intimately related to what Edwards describes, variously, as "divine discoveries," "spiritual discoveries," "gracious discoveries," "discoveries of Christ," or "discoveries of God's glory." "The sense of the heart" is not, however, synonymous with such "discoveries"; such "discoveries" certainly include "the sense of the heart" integral to regeneration, but they also surpass it. Indeed, it could be said that these "discoveries" relate to "the sense of the heart" as revival relates to regeneration; the former in each case involves a further intensification of those affections found in the latter. It is important to note at this point the significance of Edwards's concept of height or degree in the realm of spiritual experience. In *Some Thoughts Concerning the Revival,* Edwards contends that "the holiness of the heart or will is capable of being raised to a hundred times as great a degree of strength as it is in the most eminent saint on earth."[65] "Undoubtedly, there are also true, holy, and solid affections; and the higher these are raised, the better; and if they are raised to an exceeding great height, they are not to be thought meanly of or suspected, merely because of their great degree, but on the contrary to be esteemed and rejoiced in."[66] It is crucial to note that these "discoveries" are not new revelations concerning God and Christ in any objective, external sense—Edwards had no brief whatsoever for such a notion. Rather, they are unveilings of God and Christ to the soul in a subjective, internal sense. Such "discoveries" are, however, rooted and grounded in objective, external revelation. In his sermon, *The Portion of the Righteous,* Edwards demonstrates that these "discoveries" involve a view, a vision, a sight, an unveiling, not to the bodily eyes, nor to the eyes of the imagination, but to the eyes of the soul, of the God and the Christ of God revealed in the Scriptures:

> God sometimes is pleased to remove the veil, to draw the curtain, and to give the saints sweet visions. Sometimes there is, as it were, a window opened in heaven, and Christ shows himself through the lattice; they have sometimes a beam of sweet light breaking forth from above into the soul; and God and the Redeemer sometimes come to them, and make friendly visits to them, and manifest themselves to them.[67]

This veil is clearly one that separates this world from the eternal world of heaven; it is also one that separates this world from the eternal world of hell.

65. Edwards, *Great Awakening*, 298.

66. Edwards, *Great Awakening*, 299.

67. Hickman, *Works of Jonathan Edwards*, 2.889–90.

Thus it is a veil that separates humanity from God in the life and the world to come. As such, it is a concept that is marked by a certain ambivalence—the veil is, like the gospel itself, both "the savour of life unto life" and "the savour of death unto death" (2 Cor 2:26). It is, therefore, important to note that, if the concept of the veil often has a distinctly positive, blessed connotation, there are many other occasions when this concept has a distinctly negative, even terrifying connotation. Both connotations reflect Edwards's persistent preoccupation with the proximity, the accessibility, the immanence of the living God. Thus the concept of the veil has, interestingly, both a spatial and a temporal aspect in that the eternal worlds of heaven and hell are, for saint and sinner alike, only one beat of the heart away.

"THE HANDS OF GOD"

It is particularly in Edwards's evangelistic preaching that this negative, even terrifying, aspect is found. Indeed, in his pulpit ministry, Edwards makes recurrent use of the simple yet powerful theme of "the hands of God." He utilizes this theme in *Men Naturally Are God's Enemies* as he emphasizes the immediacy of the living, transcendent God:

> Consider, ye that are enemies to God, how great he is. He is the eternal God who fills heaven and earth, and whom the heaven of heavens cannot contain. He is the God that made you; in whose hand your breath is, and whose are all your ways; the God in whom you live, and move, and have your being; who has your soul and body in his hands every moment . . . God, whose enemy you are, has the frame of your body in his hands. Your times are in his hand; and he it is that appoints your bounds.[68]

Similarly, in *Procrastination, or, The Sin and Folly of Depending on Future Time*, Edwards returns to the theme of "the hands of God": "We are in God's hands; our lives are in his hands; he hath set our bounds; the number of our months and days are with him; nor hath he told them to us."[69] Again, in his celebrated *Farewell Sermon* (1750), the ousted Northampton minister moves towards his conclusion with this poignant *adieu* to his pastoral charge of the last twenty-three years: "But now I must bid you farewell: I must leave you in the hands of God."[70] Indeed, the very title of Edwards's most famous sermon, *Sinners in the Hands of an Angry God* (1741), demonstrates again

68. Hickman, *Works of Jonathan Edwards*, 2.139.
69. Hickman, *Works of Jonathan Edwards*, 2.239.
70. Edwards, *Sermons and Discourses, 1743–1758*, 483.

this persistent preoccupation with the immediacy of God: the sinner—every sinner under the sun—is continually in God's hands, not only in the life and the world to come, but now, in the present, in this life and this world, and there is but the flimsiest veil that separates him from the eternal judgment of God. In this sermon, Edwards expresses the concept of the veil by means of a very graphic metaphor: "Unconverted men," he insists, "walk over the pit of hell on a rotten covering."[71] Conrad Cherry makes this comment: "Edwards made dramatic use of everyday images to convey this sense of life's uncertainty: an insect suspended over a fire by a slender thread, men walking on a rotten covering stretched over a deep pit, a rock hurled toward a delicate spider's web."[72] These "images of the tenuousness of life,"[73] as Marsden aptly describes them, clearly cohere powerfully with Edwards's great emphasis upon the immediacy of God.

THE IMMEDIACY OF EDWARDS'S RHETORIC

It is an interesting fact that in the course of *Sinners in the Hands of an Angry God,* Edwards enhances this emphasis upon the immediacy of God via the immediacy of his rhetoric. At a certain point in the sermon, the Enfield preacher makes a very significant rhetorical transition, and a comparison between the final paragraph of the Doctrinal section and the first paragraph containing the Application highlights the startling character of this transition: Edwards moves from the more objective third person ("natural men," "they," "them") to the more subjective second person ("you," "every one of you that are out of Christ," "your"):

> The *Use* may be of *Awakening* to unconverted persons in this congregation. This that you have heard is the case of every one of you that are out of Christ. That world of misery, that lake of burning brimstone is extended abroad under you. *There* is the dreadful pit of the glowing flames of the wrath of God; there is hell's wide gaping mouth open; and you have nothing to stand upon, nor any thing to take hold of: there is nothing between you and hell but the air; 'tis only the power and mere pleasure of God that holds you up.[74]

71. Edwards, *Sermons and Discourses, 1739–1742*, 407.
72. Cherry, "Imagery and Analysis," 23.
73. Marsden, *Jonathan Edwards*, 222.
74. Edwards, *Sermons and Discourses, 1739–1742*, 409–10.

The specific rhetorical strategies utilized in the Enfield sermon have been analyzed by the literary historian, J.A. Leo Lemay:

> Jonathan Edwards achieves extraordinary tension and suspense by brilliant rhetorical strategies. The increasing immediacy of person, time, and place throughout *Sinners in the Hands of an Angry God* explains much of its escalating emotional appeal.[75]

"The personal references in the sermon gradually become more immediate," observes Lemay. "In the Use or Application section, Edwards abruptly changes from *they* to *you* . . . The increasing immediacy of personal reference helps make the sermon a persuasive rhetorical masterpiece."[76] It is, of course, "the pronominal shift"[77] involving the second person, whether the subject or the object of the verb, that generates this "increasing immediacy of person." Edwards's striking rhetorical immediacy serves, in this famous sermon, as a remarkable handmaid to his emphasis upon the immediacy of the God with whom men have to do.

"DIVINE DISCOVERIES"

It is important to note that the immediacy of God in the realm of spiritual experience has a dual aspect. "Legal convictions"[78] and "legal awakenings,"[79] Edwards noted in the 1734–1735 revival in Northampton, commonly precede "divine discoveries" and "sweet visions." This dual aspect coheres with the prediction made by the aged Simeon concerning the Christ-child: "Behold, this child is set for the fall and rising again of many in Israel" (Luke 2:34)."The fall and rising again" are evident, for instance, in the conversion of Abigail Hutchinson, a young woman in very frail health who died not long after the waning of the revival and who was one of "two particular instances"[80] of conversion highlighted by Edwards in *A Faithful Narrative*. Edwards describes this young woman as "a very eminent instance of Christian experience."[81] What, then, was her experience? Edwards emphasizes that, in the early phase of her conversion, she was characterized by "an extraordinary sense of her own sinfulness, particularly the sinfulness of her

75. Lemay, "Rhetorical Strategies," 186.
76. Lemay, "Rhetorical Strategies," 186–87.
77. Lemay, "Rhetorical Strategies," 187.
78. Edwards, *Great Awaken*ing, 166.
79. Edwards, *Great Awaken*ing, 163.
80. Edwards, *Great Awaken*ing, 191.
81. Edwards, *Great Awaken*ing, 199.

nature and wickedness of her heart."[82] These awakenings had lasted scarcely a week, however, before they gave way to the peace and joy of resting in Christ. Edwards relates:

> She had many extraordinary discoveries of the glory of God and Christ. Her mind was so swallowed up with a sense of the glory of God's truth and other perfections, that she said it seemed as though her life was going, and that she saw it was easy with God to take away her life by discoveries of himself . . . She once expressed herself to one of her sisters to this purpose, that she had continued whole days and whole nights in a constant ravishing view of the glory of God and Christ, having enjoyed as much as her life could bear.[83]

Edwards remarks that "it seemed to me she dwelt for days together in a kind of beatific vision of God; and seemed to have, as I thought, as immediate an intercourse with him as a child with a father."[84] In such discoveries, there appears even to be a certain luminosity with regard to the truths of the gospel—a luminosity in which there is an almost immediate, intuitive grasp of truth and in which faith is transmuted into a kind of sight.

Jonathan Edwards was himself no stranger to such "discoveries of Christ," and in his *Personal Narrative* (1739), he provides the following remarkable account of one such experience:

> Once, as I rid out into the woods for my health, *anno* 1737; and having lit from my horse in a retired place, as my manner commonly has been, to walk for divine contemplation and prayer; I had a view, that for me was extraordinary, of the glory of the Son of God, as mediator between God and man; and his wonderful, great, full, pure and sweet grace and love, and meek and gentle condescension. This grace that appeared to me so calm and sweet, appeared great above the heavens. The person of Christ appeared ineffably excellent, with an excellency great enough to swallow up all thought and conception. Which continued, as near as I can judge, about an hour; which kept me, the bigger part of the time, in a flood of tears, and weeping aloud. I felt withal, an ardency of soul to be, what I know not otherwise how to express, than to be emptied and annihilated; to lie in the dust, and to be full of Christ alone; to love him with a holy and pure love; to trust in him; to live upon him; to serve and follow him,

82. Edwards, *Great Awakening*, 192.

83. Edwards, *Great Awakening*, 194, 195.

84. Edwards, *Great Awakening*, 195.

> and to be perfectly sanctified and made pure, with a divine and heavenly purity. I have several other times, had views very much of the same nature, and that have had the same effects.[85]

SARAH EDWARDS

But Edwards's *pièce de résistance* in the realm of "divine discoveries" is, surely, his account of the extraordinary experiences of his wife, Sarah, both prior to and during the Great Awakening. Referring to her as "the person" for the sake of anonymity and modesty, Edwards describes his wife's remarkable spiritual experiences in considerable detail:

> And in the highest transports of any of the instances that I have been acquainted with, and where the affections of admiration, love and joy, . . . have been raised to a higher pitch than in any other instances I have observed or been informed of, the following things have been united: *viz.* a very frequent dwelling, for some considerable time together, in views of the glory of the divine perfections and Christ's excellencies, that the soul in the meantime has been as it were perfectly overwhelmed, and swallowed up with light and love and a sweet solace, rest and joy of soul, that was altogether unspeakable; and more than once continuing for five or six hours together, without any interruption, in that clear and lively view or sense of the infinite beauty and amiableness of Christ's person, and the heavenly sweetness of his transcendent love; so that (to use the person's own expressions) the soul remained in a kind of heavenly Elysium, and did as it were swim in the rays of Christ's love, like a little mote swimming in the beams of the sun, or streams of his light that come in at a window; and the heart was swallowed up in a kind of glow of Christ's love, coming down from Christ's heart in heaven, as a constant stream of sweet light, at the same time the soul all flowing out in love to him; so that there seemed to be a constant flowing and reflowing from heart to heart. The soul dwelt on high, and was lost in God, and seemed almost to leave the body; dwelling in a pure delight that fed and satisfied the soul; enjoying pleasure without the least sting, or any interruption, a sweetness that the soul was lost in; . . . and the like heavenly delight and unspeakable joy of soul, enjoyed from time to time, for years together.[86]

85. Edwards, *Letters and Personal Writings*, 801.

86. Edwards, *Great Awaken*ing, 332.

It is interesting to note at this point that there is a kind of effervescence in Edwards's theology and experience. This effervescence is evident in his remarkable doctrine of *creatio continua;* it is also evident in Edwards's *apologia* for his wife's remarkable spiritual experiences, as represented in the vocabulary of flux and reflux: "so that there seemed to be a constant flowing and reflowing from heart to heart." There is immediacy here; there is intimacy here; there is spiritual intercourse; there is a kind of *ekstasis.* Indeed, Sarah Edwards's experience is cast in language that contains overtones of the erotic.

This remarkable description of his wife's spiritual experience is also reminiscent of the language of "emanation and remanation" in *God's Chief End in Creation* (1765):

> In the creature's knowing, esteeming, loving, rejoicing in, and praising God, the glory of God is both exhibited and acknowledged; his fullness is received and returned. Here is both an *emanation* and *remanation.* The refulgence shines upon and into the creature, and is reflected back to the luminary. The beams of glory come from God, are something of God, and are refunded back again to their original. So that the whole is *of* God, and *in* God, and *to* God; and God is the beginning, middle and end in this affair.[87]

We note, once again, a certain correlation in Edwards's thought between his views in the sphere of spiritual experience and his views in the sphere of God and the creation. The language of emanationism is, interestingly, common to his treatment of both spheres. Edwards's doctrine of the Spirit of God is clearly a powerfully dynamic doctrine, and the dynamic character of his doctrine is inseparably related to the sovereignty and the immediacy of the Spirit's operations and is reflected in this emanationist strand in his thought. We note here what Strobel has described as "the continuum of emanation to remanation."[88] "God's emanation is effectual for remanation, so that redemption entails participation, through Christ, in the beatific-delight of God."[89]

These experiences on the part of Abigail Hutchinson, Jonathan Edwards, and Sarah Edwards are striking examples of what Edwards himself describes as "God's removing the veil," "his drawing the curtain," and "giving the saints sweet visions." "A window is, as it were, opened in heaven, and Christ shows himself through the lattice." Such are "the beams of sweet light breaking forth from above into the soul," such are the "friendly visits"

87. Edwards, *Ethical Writings*, 531.

88. Strobel, *Reinterpretation*, 209.

89. Strobel, *Reinterpretation*, 104.

made by God and the Redeemer to the souls of his saints, and such is "the manifestation of God" unto them. Elsewhere, Edwards describes these "friendly visits" as "foretastes of heaven"[90] or "prelibations of heaven's glory given upon earth."[91] Edwards's view of the immediacy of God is such that he sees the worlds of both heaven and hell as impinging powerfully, through the veil, upon this present world.

REVIVAL

We have noted that the "divine discoveries" experienced by Abigail Hutchinson, Jonathan Edwards, and Sarah Edwards cohere with Edwards's theology of revival. Revival is to the church what "divine discoveries" are to the individual—in each of these there is a definite quickening that occurs. Widely regarded as "the theologian of revival," Edwards experienced revival twice: firstly, in the awakening in Northampton and the Connecticut River Valley from 1734 to 1735; secondly, in the Great Awakening from 1740 to 1742. Edwards's classic definition of revival is found in *A History of the Work of Redemption* (1774):

> It may here be observed that from the fall of man to this day wherein we live the Work of Redemption in its effect has mainly been carried on by remarkable pourings out of the Spirit of God. Though there be a more constant influence of God's Spirit always in some degree attending his ordinances, yet the way in which the greatest things have been done towards carrying on this work always has been by remarkable pourings out of the Spirit at special seasons of mercy.[92]

The crucial phrase here is this: "remarkable pourings out of the Spirit at special seasons of mercy." There is, Edwards insists, "a more constant influence of God's Spirit always in some degree attending his ordinances"; but there are also times and seasons when God pours out his Spirit in great and remarkable measure. Thus there is an ebb and flow in the Spirit's operations. Integral to Edwards's view of revival is the concept of periodicity and the concept of degree—there are certain times and seasons when the Spirit of God is poured forth, and the actual measure of the Spirit thus communicated varies from one revival to another. For Edwards, revival is nothing less than an outpouring of the Spirit, a special season of mercy, a remarkable

90. Edwards, *Great Awakening*, 232.

91. Edwards, *Great Awakening*, 346.

92. Edwards, *Work of Redemption*, 143.

effusion or communication of the Third Person of the Godhead. Revival is thus a manifestation of both the sovereignty and the immediacy of God.

It is also important to note that there is a crucial connection between Edwards's emphasis upon divine immediacy and his Trinitarianism. It is not that a Trinitarian theology guarantees an emphasis upon divine immediacy—there have clearly been many in the long history of the Christian church who have been unreservedly Trinitarian in their theology, yet have lacked such an emphasis. It is rather that it is almost inconceivable that an emphasis upon the immediacy of God should be found in the anti-Trinitarian. The natural tendency of anti-Trinitarianism is towards Unitarianism, which is, in the final analysis, simply a more respectable, quasi-religious version of deism. Unitarianism, which by definition denies the deity of the Son and the Spirit, inevitably distances God from the world. By contrast, Trinitarianism, with its doctrine of the incarnation of Christ and its concept of the outpouring of the Spirit, is conducive to a strong emphasis upon the immediacy of God.

One of the most striking elements both in Edwards's accounts and in his theology of revival is his emphasis upon the presence of God. In *A Faithful Narrative,* Edwards gives this description of the awakening in Northampton:

> This work of God . . . soon made a glorious alteration in the town; so that in the spring and summer following, *anno* 1735, the town seemed to be full of the presence of God: it never was so full of love, nor so full of joy; and yet so full of distress, as it was then. There were remarkable tokens of God's presence in almost every house.[93]

As he concludes his narrative, Edwards makes this observation concerning the blessing of God upon the town of Northampton: "And we are evidently a people blessed of the Lord! And here, in this corner of the world, God dwells and manifests his glory."[94] The presence of God in view here is, obviously, something that goes beyond the fact of his omnipresence. The great God that is, throughout the inconceivably vast reaches of the universe, omnipresent, the God that is at all times and in all places immediately present, is also the God who, at special times and seasons, manifests his presence in an unusual manner and to an extraordinary degree. This presence is, clearly, a localized presence; it is a special presence; and it is inextricably linked with the outpouring of the Spirit of God. Throughout his writings, whether in treatise or in sermon, Edwards emphasizes that at such times, "God appears

93. Edwards, *Great Awakening*, 151.

94. Edwards, *Great Awakening*, 210.

unusually present."[95] "God . . . is then extraordinarily present."[96] "Again, the time of the strivings of God's Spirit is more precious than other time. That is the time when God is near."[97] The deist was profoundly committed to the concept of God's absence from the world; Jonathan Edwards was profoundly committed to the concept of God's presence in the world.

ANTI-IMMEDIACY

But the presence of God in revival, so manifestly obvious to Edwards, was denied by others at the time of the Great Awakening. It is interesting to note how often, throughout *Thoughts on the Revival,* Edwards sounds an alarm against the anti-immediacy impulse, deistic or (perhaps we should say) Unitarian in tendency, of the opponents of the Great Awakening. The grand representative of this opposition to the revival was Charles Chauncy (1705–87), the minister of the First Church in Boston. During the Great Awakening, Chauncy began to collect information concerning the alleged excesses of the revival from newspapers, *via* correspondence with friends, and by means of a grand tour of New England, New York, and New Jersey. In 1743, this champion of decorum and good order published his *Seasonable Thoughts on the State of Religion in New England.* Thus, if opposition to the enthusiasts constituted one of the battle-fronts for Edwards, opposition to rationalists such as Charles Chauncy constituted the other. In the following cogent passage, Edwards adduces the example of David's wife, Michal, as a counterblast to Chauncy's position:

> But we read of one of David's wives, even Michal, Saul's daughter, whose heart was not engaged in the affair, and did not appear with others to rejoice and praise God on this occasion, but kept away and stood at a distance, as disaffected and disliking the management; she despised and ridiculed the transports and extraordinary manifestations of joy that then were; and the curse that she brought upon herself by it was that of being barren to the day of her death . . . Let this be a warning to us: let us take heed, in this day of the bringing up of the ark of God, that while we are in visibility and profession the spouse of the spiritual David, we do not shew ourselves to be indeed the children of false-hearted and rebellious Saul, by our standing aloof, and our not joining in the joy and praises of the day, and disliking

95. Edwards, *Great Awakening*, 395.

96. Edwards, *Great Awakening*, 395.

97. Edwards, *Sermons and Discourses, 1734–1738*, 259.

> and despising the joys and affections of God's people, because they are to so high a degree, and so bring the curse of perpetual barrenness upon our souls.[98]

The *leitmotiv* employed here and elsewhere by Edwards is that of "standing aloof," "lying still," "keeping silence," "standing by as an indifferent spectator," and "standing at a distance." "All persons will greatly expose themselves to the curse of God, by opposing, or standing at a distance, and keeping silence at such a time as this."[99] Indeed, Edwards regarded this "standing at a distance" as a manifestation of "Arminian principles"—such a stance was essentially deistic in tendency. Indeed, in *Some Thoughts Concerning the Revival,* Edwards beseeches those that had been "inclining to Arminian principles" to consider "whether any good medium can be found, where a man can rest with any stability, between owning this work, and being a Deist . . . Now is a good time for Arminians to change their principles."[100] By "Arminian principles," Edwards intends that incipient rationalism that characterized men such as Charles Chauncy and Jonathan Mayhew, both ministers in Boston. Edwards's reasoning here is essentially as follows: to deny the reality and the power of such a palpable work of the Spirit is, in effect, to deny the reality and the power of the Spirit himself, and thus to drift very subtly, but inevitably, away from a Trinitarian and towards a Unitarian position. C.C. Goen observes:

> With remarkable prescience, Edwards foresaw that the Great Awakening was to become a decisive watershed in American religious thought. As history would eventually reveal, many of the rationalistic opposers of the revival were really pre-Unitarians who would develop an ever more self-conscious antithesis to evangelicalism until the result could fairly be called Deism.[101]

Elwood notes the battle on two fronts waged by Edwards with regard to spiritual experience—it was a battle against the deists on the one hand and against the enthusiasts on the other:

> The deists were reducing religion to the rationally demonstrable, squeezing out its mystical element. The "Enthusiasts," on the other side, were appealing to irrational emotions. In opposition to the antimystical rationalism of the deists as well as to the nonmystical intellectualism of orthodox Puritanism, Edwards

98. Edwards, *Great Awakening*, 366.

99. Edwards, *Great Awakening*, 368.

100. Edwards, *Great Awakening*, 503.

101. Edwards, *Great Awakening*, 78.

> affirmed that "true religion, in great part, consists in the affections" . . . In an "age of reason" he dared to assert—without, however, appealing to unreasoned emotions—that the "heart" is "the principle and original seat" of religious consciousness, for emotions are "the spring of men's actions."[102]

It should be noted, therefore, that there is a significant mystical element in Edwards. He eschews not only "the antimystical rationalism of the deists," but also "the nonmystical intellectualism of orthodox Puritanism," and embraces what B.B. Warfield describes as a "Christian mysticism,"[103] or what might, alternatively, be described as a kind of mystical Calvinism—a mystical Calvinism that, far from substituting religious experience for the objective revelation of the written Word, is rooted and grounded in the external authority of that Word and insists upon the closest conjunction of the Word and the Spirit.

THE IMMEDIACY SPECTRUM

It is interesting to note that there is, within the broad range of eighteenth-century religion, a fascinating spectrum with regard to the issue of the immediacy of God and the related issue of the immediacy of the soul's approach to God—a spectrum that ranges from the anti-immediacy position of the deist to the ultra-immediacy position of the enthusiast: the "absentee landlord" concept of rationalistic deism, the sacramentalist sacerdotalism of Roman Catholicism, the evangelical Protestantism of the Word-and-Spirit approach of conservative Puritanism, the undue emphasis upon the Holy Spirit in radical Puritanism, and the dangerous "inner light" doctrine of Quakerism—these are the various *foci* within the broad spectrum of positions that relate to the issue of the immediacy of God. Edwards's position is clearly that of the Word-and-Spirit approach of conservative Puritanism; indeed, Edwards has been described by Perry Miller as "the archconservator of the Puritan past."[104] It should be noted, therefore, that his inveterate opposition to the deistic distancing of God is balanced by his inveterate opposition to the enthusiasm of the radical Puritans and the Quakers. Edwards's position was, therefore, that of the *via media* of conservative Puritanism, but it was a *via media* with a very powerful yet measured emphasis upon the immediate influence of the Spirit of God.

102. Elwood, *Philosophical Theology*, 113–14.

103. Warfield, "Mysticism and Christianity," 654.

104. Miller, *Errand into the Wilderness*, 167.

THE EXPERIMENTAL NOTE

It is important to note the general character and tendency of the conservative Puritanism espoused by Edwards. Of particular significance is the experimental aspect within the Puritan tradition: "What is new," observes Nuttall, "is the place given in Puritan exposition to experience."[105] It should be noted that, if Puritanism is approached from a priestly direction, any movement away from sacerdotalism and sacramentalism will inevitably be a movement towards immediacy. The historical movement in the sixteenth and seventeenth centuries from the Church of Rome to Anglicanism, and from Anglicanism to Puritanism is, therefore, a movement towards immediacy in relation to God. The sacerdotal, the hierarchical, the external, the liturgical, the formal, and the visible elements recede, and the personal, the private, the internal, the vital, the experimental, and the invisible elements tend to come to the fore. It is an interesting and irrefutable fact that personal religion, private religion—what Edwards persistently describes, variously, as "vital religion," "heart religion," or "experimental piety"—always has a more immediate air than sacramentalist sacerdotalism, whether Roman, Anglican, or Lutheran. In such a religion, human mediators recede and the divine-human Mediator comes to the fore, providing access to God and highlighting God's accessibility and immediacy.

It is an interesting fact, however, that Edwards's emphasis upon divine immediacy in the sphere of spiritual experience is marked by somewhat less exuberance and somewhat greater restraint than his emphasis upon divine immediacy in the sphere of God and the creation. If there is, in the latter sphere, something quite radical about his views on divine immediacy, there is something quite conservative about his views on divine immediacy in the sphere of spiritual experience—he has no brief for the enthusiasm of the Anabaptists, the Quakers, or the radical Puritans. This relative conservatism is demonstrated by the fact of his many strictures with regard to "false discoveries" and the ultra-supernaturalism of the enthusiasts. Edwards does not succumb to what he himself indicts in *Distinguishing Marks* (1741) as "enthusiastic wildness and extravagance."[106] It is a very significant fact that there is, in this treatise, a definite sobriety about the positive marks of a work of the Spirit of God adduced by Edwards. He specifies *inter alia* an increase in one's esteem of Jesus as the Son of God and the Savior of humanity, an increase in one's regard for the Holy Scriptures, and an increase in a spirit of love to God and humanity.[107] Thus

105. Nuttall, *Holy Spirit*, 7.

106. Edwards, *Great Awakening*, 270.

107. See Edwards, *Great Awakening*, 248–59.

Edwards rejects, both in principle and in practice, the more extremist elements that might conceivably have accompanied a strong emphasis upon divine immediacy in this sphere. The great factor in this restraint is, surely, the external, objective authority of the Word of God. Edwards did not, as was the manner of some, try the Word by the Spirit, but the Spirit by the Word.[108]

Nevertheless, it is undeniable that there is, throughout Edwards's *oeuvre,* an extremely powerful experimental, experiential thrust. Edwards's central thesis in *Religious Affections* is this: "True religion, in great part, consists in holy affections."[109] His constant emphasis upon "holy affections," "vital religion," "heart religion," "experimental piety," "the sense of the heart," "divine discoveries," "the influences of the Spirit," "the presence of God," and "revival" demonstrates a profound preoccupation on his part with private, personal Christianity. It is an emphasis that is, by definition, conducive to a species of Christianity that has a distinctly immediate air. What, then, of the charge by the covenant theologian, Peter Y. De Jong, that Edwards is characterized by "Anabaptist individualistic piety"?[110] In view of Edwards's persistent critique of the Anabaptists and the Quakers, there would appear to be some injustice in the charge; nevertheless, the charge contains an important element of truth. There is no vestige of hypercovenantism[111] in Edwards's theology; indeed, there is little or no emphasis upon the covenantal solidarity of the Christian family in his theology. His powerfully experimental theology is, indeed, highly individualistic, and this very individualism coheres with and enhances the related concepts of the immediacy of God and the immediacy of the soul's approach to God. Edwards's theology is one that is marked by the powerful conjunction of both Word and Spirit—in this, Edwards reveals himself as a loyal son of the Reformed tradition: "'Wort und Geist' ist die Parole der Reformation" ("'Word and Spirit' is the watchword of the Reformation").[112] Edwards's theology of the external, objective authority of the Word is such that it exercises a significant control of his theology of the Spirit; but his theology of the immediate influence of the Spirit is such that it delivers his theology of the Word from a potentially arid, over-intellectual Calvinism and lends it a vigor, a vitality, a warmth, a reality, indeed, a dynamism that, within the conservative Puritan tradition, has perhaps few peers.

108. "Throughout the years from 1650 onwards there is a perpetual controversy, whether the Word is to be tried by the Spirit, or the Spirit by the Word." Nuttall, *Holy Spirit*, 28.

109. Edwards, *Religious Affections*, 95.

110. De Jong, *Covenant Idea*, 116.

111. See Young, "Historic Calvinism and Neo-Calvinism" (1974).

112. See Nuttall, *Holy Spirit*, 21.

CONCLUSION

It is part of the enduring fascination of Jonathan Edwards that he was born into an era of intellectual and religious history that was characterized, quite remarkably, by the atrophy of the concept of God as First Cause. This atrophy of the concept of divine immediacy is, of course, inextricably connected with the rise of the deism that had emerged in England in the 1690s, with its insistence upon the self-subsistence and the self-sustentation of the universe, and it is crucial to note that Edwards's philosophy and his theology constitute, in very large part, a recoil from and a counterblast to this deism. Deism, Newtonianism, Materialism, Arminianism, Libertarianism, Stoddardism, incipient Unitarianism—these were the contemporary belief systems that Edwards faced on both sides of the Atlantic; they were systems that, in various ways, distanced God from the universe, from humanity, and from the church. More specifically, Edwards's counterblast to this atrophying trend was, as we have seen, that of highlighting, in a quite extraordinary manner, the very immediacy of God. Indeed, a very powerful case can be made that this theme of divine immediacy is, in fact, the Ariadne's thread that winds and wends its way through the labyrinth of Edwards's multiple philosophical, theological, ecclesiological, and experiential interests.

Although there is in general a reasonableness about Edwards's nevertheless powerful emphasis upon divine immediacy in the realm of the will, ecclesiology, and spiritual experience, there is also, surely, something exaggerated and excessive about his emphasis upon divine immediacy in the realm of God and the creation. It is interesting to note that, while Edwards did not believe in continuous revelation, he did believe in continuous creation. This latter belief is susceptible to the charge of ultra-supernaturalism on his part (just as the former belief would have been, if entertained), and it constitutes, in the sheer counter-intuitiveness that attaches to it, a species of metaphysical enthusiasm. Indeed, it would not be improper to contend that, notwithstanding his claim that this doctrine is taught in the Scriptures, Edwards's position with regard to continuous creation falls, uncharacteristically, under the category of what Locke aptly describes as "the ungrounded fancies of a man's own brain."

In short, Edwards's response to the general atrophy of the concept of divine immediacy was that of producing a philosophical-theological system that is characterized, in one particular sphere—that of God and the creation—by the hypertrophy of this concept. Moreover, it is undeniable that the hypertrophy of the concept of divine immediacy in this particular sphere creates real (albeit not necessarily insuperable) difficulties with regard to the internal coherence of his system, as in the juxtaposition of his determinism and his occasionalism. The greatest problem that emerges from his continuous creation-*cum*-occasionalism system, however, is that this system appears to destroy all mundane causation, it appears to negate the moral responsibility of humanity, and it appears to render God both the author and the actor of sin.

There can be little doubt that Jonathan Edwards was profoundly provoked by deism; there can also be little doubt that, in his recoil from deism, Edwards has overreacted significantly at certain specific points and has veered to the opposite extreme of a panentheizing theology. Thus the Deity *in absentia* of the deists is now replaced by a God, whose immediacy is significantly hypertrophied, and God is construed by Edwards as all-encircling, all-comprehending, ever re-creating all things *ex nihilo* at every successive moment. It should be noted that, while the God of deism creates the universe and then, as it were, releases it, Edwards's God causes the universe to flow forth from himself, and he, as it were, takes it up into himself. The net result is panentheism. Certainly, panentheism is not pantheism; but panentheism shares with pantheism a number of the problems intrinsic to the latter: in Edwards's doctrine of continuous creation there is a blurring of the distinction between the First Cause and second causes; there is also, inevitably, in this scheme a blurring of the distinction between the supernatural and the natural. If all things are created *de novo ex nihilo* at every successive moment, as Edwards insists in *Original Sin*, then nothing is natural—all is supernatural. But if all is supernatural and nothing is natural, there is a sense in which all is natural and nothing is supernatural—the natural and the supernatural are fused, and the distinction between them is destroyed.

On July 5, 1750, not long after his pastoral relationship of twenty-three years with the people of Northampton had been dissolved and at a time when, understandably, he would perhaps be seeking a ministerial call elsewhere, possibly even to Scotland, Edwards wrote to the Rev. John Erskine in Kirkintilloch, near Glasgow, indicating his disillusionment with what he described as "our unsettled, independent, confused way of church government" in New England Congregationalism.[1] In his letter, he stated that he would have no difficulty in affirming his acceptance of the formularies of the Church of Scotland: "As to my subscribing to the substance of the Westminster Confession, there would be no difficulty."[2] What is so remarkable here is not that New England's leading Congregationalist preacher-theologian should tip his hand in the direction of Presbyterianism, but rather that a *de facto* occasionalist-panentheist should apparently feel so ready and able to endorse the Westminster Confession of Faith. The stance of the Westminster Standards on the issue of primary and secondary causation is quite clear—the Westminster Confession of Faith makes a decisive distinction between (on the one hand) "the First Cause," whose operations are supremely evident in the initial creation, in providential interventions, and also in miracles, and (on the other hand) "second causes" or "means," by which God ordinarily governs and sustains the cosmos. Edwards's *de facto* suppression—indeed, his effective dissolution—of second causes, mechanism, and means demonstrates that there is, in fact, a chasm between his *de facto* position in this matter and the *de jure* position of the Westminster Confession of Faith. What is, perhaps, most startling of all, however, is the seemingly complete lack of awareness of this chasm on Edwards's part.

These flaws do not appear to be deliberate or willful on Edwards's part—rather, they appear to be unintentional and inadvertent. They are, it seems, the unseen ramifications and corollaries of Edwards's stated positions and constitute, perhaps, a good example of "the law of unintended consequence." These problems are, however, clearly not minor problems; indeed, they introduce major difficulties into certain parts of his system. Moreover, the fact that such a precise, meticulous thinker as Jonathan Edwards, with his hawk-like eye for the slightest logical inconsistency, either did not grasp or was not concerned about these problems is quite extraordinary. Thus, if the concept of divine immediacy is the Ariadne's thread that runs throughout the massive, multifaceted corpus of Edwards's thought, his *malebranchiste* endorsement of the concept of occasionalism is, surely, the Achilles' heel of his entire philosophical-theological system.

1. Edwards, *Letters and Personal Writings*, 355.
2. Edwards, *Letters and Personal Writings*, 355.

It is, however, very important that, in calling attention to these flaws in Edwards's system, we should not fail to note Edwards's very considerable accomplishment with regard to the concept of the immediacy of God. It is this theme of divine immediacy that connects so closely in Edwards's mind multiple interests and themes within the different spheres of creation, the will, ecclesiology, and spiritual experience. More precisely, this theme of divine immediacy binds together interests and themes as apparently diverse as the following: God's knowledge, God's atemporality; God's power, continuous creation; God's transcendence, God's immanence; deism, mechanism, self-subsistence, autonomy; body, solidity, indivisibility, resistance, motion, gravity, existence itself; occasionalism, the doctrine of temporal parts; emanationism, the divinizing of the creation; cosmic autonomy, human autonomy; determinism, means, causality, the First Cause, second causes; the preservation of the cosmos, the illusory nature of reality; hamartiology; regeneration, instantaneousness, gradualism; Trinitarianism; Libertarianism; ecclesiastical purity, "the New England experiment," the Halfway Covenant, Stoddardism, Arminianism; "moral sincerity," "historical faith," nominal Christianity, "gracious sincerity"; *fiducia*, the consent of the will, "the heart"; ultra-supernaturalism, Quakerism, "the light within"; ultra-immediacy, anti-immediacy; "the veil," "divine discoveries"; "the sense of the heart," "speculative knowledge," "sensible knowledge"; experimental religion, individualistic piety, the sense of taste, "the sixth sense," the beauty of the person and work of Christ, the supernatural; revival, effusions of the Spirit, the absence of God, the presence of God, the Great Awakening; Unitarianism; objective revelation, subjective inspiration; Word and Spirit, the common influences of the Spirit; rhetorical immediacy, "the hands of God," the tenuousness of life; the luminous, the numinous, the beatific vision, mystical Calvinism; externality, the externalization of religion, the externalization of God. All of these themes, whether considered positively or negatively by Edwards, are connected by the thread of divine immediacy. Indeed, there is, in Edwards's thought as a whole, a fundamental ubiquity and inescapability about this theme of the immediacy of God.

"The real life of Jonathan Edwards," observes Perry Miller, "was the life of his mind."[3] This statement by Miller is a tribute to the extraordinary intellectual powers of the eighteenth-century New England thinker who is widely regarded as America's greatest philosopher and her greatest theologian. It is, surely, part of the genius of Jonathan Edwards that throughout his multiple and varied interests of a philosophical, theological, ecclesiological, and experiential nature—indeed, throughout his preaching

3. Miller, *Jonathan Edwards*, xi.

also—there runs this fundamental motif, this principle of coherence and correlation; namely, that of the immediacy of God. Thus as Edwards responds to very varied intellectual and spiritual issues at very different levels—whether it be the adducing of a doctrine of *creatio continua* in support of an arbitrary divine constitution of the oneness of Adam's posterity or whether it be the fact that sinners under judgment are, at all times, in "the hands of God"; whether it be the issue of the purity of the church in the sacraments or whether it be the role of "the sense of the heart" in regeneration—it is this ubiquitous theme, this omnipresent thread, that we encounter. Edwards's extremely powerful theocentrism has been widely acknowledged. What is not so widely recognized is the radical role played within his theocentrism by the concept of God as First Cause. Edwards's calculated response to the deistic relocating of God in the late seventeenth and early eighteenth century was that of relocating the relocated God; his response, however, did not involve a return to the *status quo ante* (the state of affairs as it was before). In Edwards's hands, second causes recede, indeed, they virtually disappear, and God the great First Cause, God the great continuing Creator, is brought out of the dim recesses of time and space in deism and placed at the very forefront of the universe. In the final analysis, what is so remarkable about Edwards's thought is his vision of what has been described as "the immanence of the transcendent"[4]—his vision of what Edwards himself describes as "the reality, the vastness, and infinite importance, and nearness of spiritual and eternal things"[5]—in short, his vision of the sheer immediateness of the living God. It is a quite extraordinary vision.

4. See Elwood, *Philosophical Theology*, 19.

5. Edwards, *Great Awakening*, 320.

BIBLIOGRAPHY

PRIMARY SOURCES

The Yale Edition of Edwards's Works

Jonathan Edwards. *The Works of Jonathan Edwards*. Vol. 1, *Freedom of the Will*. Edited by Paul Ramsey. New Haven: Yale University Press, 1957.

———. *The Works of Jonathan Edwards*. Vol. 2, *Religious Affections*. Edited by John Smith. New Haven: Yale University Press, 1959.

———. *The Works of Jonathan Edwards*. Vol. 3, *Original Sin*. Edited by Clyde A. Holbrook. New Haven: Yale University Press, 1970.

———. *The Works of Jonathan Edwards*. Vol. 4, *The Great Awakening*. Edited by C.C. Goen. New Haven: Yale University Press, 1972.

———. *The Works of Jonathan Edwards*. Vol. 5, *Apocalyptic Writings*. Edited by Stephen J. Stein. New Haven: Yale University Press, 1977.

———. *Scientific and Philosophical Writings*. Vol. 6, *The Works of Jonathan Edwards*. Edited by Wallace E. Anderson. New Haven: Yale University Press, 1980.

———. *The Life of David Brainerd*. Vol. 7, *The Works of Jonathan Edwards*. Edited by Norman Pettit. New Haven: Yale University Press, 1984.

———. *The Works of Jonathan Edwards*. Vol. 8, *Ethical Writings*. Edited by Paul Ramsey. New Haven: Yale University Press, 1989.

———. *The Works of Jonathan Edwards*. Vol. 9, *A History of the Work of Redemption*. Edited by John F. Wilson. New Haven: Yale University Press, 1989.

———. *The Works of Jonathan Edwards*. Vol. 10, *Sermons and Discourses, 1720–1723*. Edited by Wilson. H. Kimnach. New Haven: Yale University Press, 1992.

———. *The Works of Jonathan Edwards*. Vol. 11, *Typological Writings*. Edited by Wallace E. Anderson and David Watters. New Haven: Yale University Press, 1993.

———. *The Works of Jonathan Edwards*. Vol. 12, *Ecclesiastical Writings*. Edited by David D. Hall. New Haven: Yale University Press, 1994.

———. *The Works of Jonathan Edwards*. Vol. 13, *The "Miscellanies": a–500*. Edited by Thomas A. Schafer. New Haven: Yale University Press, 1994.

———. *The Works of Jonathan Edwards*. Vol. 14, *Sermons and Discourses, 1723–1729*. Edited by Kenneth P. Minkema. New Haven: Yale University Press, 1997.
———. *The Works of Jonathan Edwards*. Vol. 15, *Notes on Scripture*. Edited by Stephen J. Stein. New Haven: Yale University Press, 1998.
———. *The Works of Jonathan Edwards*. Vol. 16, *Letters and Personal Writings*. Edited by George S. Claghorn. New Haven: Yale University Press, 1998.
———. *The Works of Jonathan Edwards*. Vol. 17, *Sermons and Discourses*, 1730–1733. Edited by Mark Valeri. New Haven: Yale University Press, 1999.
———. *The Works of Jonathan Edwards*. Vol. 18, *The "Miscellanies": 501–832*. Edited by Ava Chamberlain. New Haven: Yale University Press, 2000.
———. *Sermons and Discourses*, 1734–38, *The Works of Jonathan Edwards*, vol. 19. Edited by M. X. Lesser. New Haven: Yale University Press, 2001.
———. *The Works of Jonathan Edwards*. Vol. 20, *The "Miscellanies": 833–1132*. Edited by Amy Plantinga-Pauw. New Haven: Yale University Press, 2002.
———. *The Works of Jonathan Edwards*. Vol. 21, *Writings on the Trinity, Grace, and Faith*. Edited by Sang Hyun Lee. New Haven: Yale University Press, 2002.
———. *The Works of Jonathan Edwards*. Vol. 22, *Sermons and Discourses, 1739–1742*. Edited by Harry S. Stout and Nathan O. Hatch. New Haven: Yale University Press, 2003.
———. *The Works of Jonathan Edwards*. Vol. 23, *The "Miscellanies": 1153–1360*. Edited by Douglas A. Sweeney. New Haven: Yale University Press, 2004.
———. *The Works of Jonathan Edwards*. Vol. 24, *The Blank Bible*. Edited by Stephen J. Stein. New Haven: Yale University Press, 2006.
———. *The Works of Jonathan Edwards*. Vol. 25, *Sermons and Discourses, 1743–1758*. Edited by Wilson H. Kimnach. New Haven: Yale University Press, 2006.
———. *The Works of Jonathan Edwards*. Vol. 26, *Catalogue of Books*. Edited by Peter J. Theusen. New Haven: Yale University Press, 2008.

The Hickman Edition of Edwards's Works

Edwards, Jonathan. *The Works of Jonathan Edwards*. 2 vols. Edited by Edward Hickman. Edinburgh: Banner of Truth, 1974 [1834].

SECONDARY SOURCES

Augustine of Hippo. *Confessions*. Translated by R.S. Pine-Coffin. London: Penguin, 1961.
———. *The Literal Meaning of Genesis*, vol. 1. Edited and translated by John Hammond Taylor. New York: Newman, 1982.
Bavinck, Herman. *The Doctrine of God*. Grand Rapids, MI: Eerdmans, 1951.
Berkhof, Louis. *Systematic Theology*. Edinburgh: Banner of Truth, 1958.
Boethius. *The Consolation of Philosophy*. Translated by Victor Watts. London: Penguin, 1999.
Cherry, Conrad. "Imagery and Analysis: Jonathan Edwards on Revivals of Religion." In *Jonathan Edwards: His Life and Influence*, edited by Charles Angoff, 19–28. Cranbury, NJ: Associated University Presses, Inc., 1975.

Cooper, John W. *Panentheism: The Other God of the Philosophers—From Plato to the Present*. Grand Rapids, MI: Baker Academic, 2006.

Cragg, Gerald R. *The Church and the Age of Reason, 1648–1789*. Grand Rapids, MI: Eerdmans, 1960.

Crisp, Oliver D. *Jonathan Edwards among the Theologians*. Grand Rapids, MI: Eerdmans, 2015.

———. *Jonathan Edwards and the Metaphysics of Sin*. Burlington, VT: Ashgate, 2005.

———. *Jonathan Edwards on God and Creation*. New York: Oxford University Press, 2012.

———. "Jonathan Edwards' Panentheism." In *Jonathan Edwards as Contemporary: Essays in Honor of Sang Hyun Lee*, edited by Don Schweitzer, 107–25. New York: Peter Lang, 2010.

Daniel, Stephen H. "Edwards' Occasionalism." In *Jonathan Edwards as Contemporary: Essays in Honor of Sang Hyun Lee*, edited by Don Schweitzer, 1–14. New York: Peter Lang, 2010.

De Jong, Peter Y. *The Covenant Idea in New England Theology, 1620–1847*. Grand Rapids, MI: Eerdmans, 1945.

Elwood, Douglas J. *The Philosophical Theology of Jonathan Edwards*. New York: Columbia University Press, 1960.

Fiering, Norman. *Jonathan Edwards's Moral Thought and Its British Context*. Chapel Hill, NC: University of North Carolina Press, 1981.

Helm, Paul. *Eternal God: A Study of God without Time*. Oxford: Clarendon, 1988.

———. "Eternity and Vision in Boethius." *European Journal for Philosophy of Religion* 1 (2009) 77–97.

———. *Faith and Understanding*. Grand Rapids, MI: Eerdmans, 1997.

———. "A Forensic Dilemma: John Locke and Jonathan Edwards on Personal Identity." In *Jonathan Edwards: Philosophical Theologian*, edited Paul Helm and Oliver D. Crisp, 45–59. Aldershot, UK: Ashgate, 2003.

———. "John Locke and Jonathan Edwards: A Reconsideration." *Journal of the History of Philosophy* 7, no. 1 (1969) 51–61.

Hindmarsh, D. Bruce. "The Reception of Jonathan Edwards by Early Evangelicals in England." In *Jonathan Edwards at Home and Abroad: Historical Memories, Cultural Movements, Global Horizons*, edited by David W. Kling and Douglas A. Sweeney, 201–21. Columbia: University of South Carolina Press, 2003.

Hodge, Charles. *Systematic Theology*. 3 vols. Grand Rapids, MI: Eerdmans, 1977.

Knox, Ronald A. *Enthusiasm: A Chapter in the History of Religion*. New York: Oxford University Press, 1950.

Lee, Sang Hyun. *The Philosophical Theology of Jonathan Edwards*. Princeton, NJ: Princeton University Press, 1988.

Leibniz, Gottfried Wilhelm. "Letter to Des Bosses, August 19, 1715." In *Philosophical Papers and Letters*, 2nd ed., edited and translated by Leroy E. Loemker. Dordrecht, Holland: Reidel, 1969.

Lemay, J.A. Leo. "Rhetorical Strategies in Sinners in the Hands of an Angry God and Narrative of the Late Massacres in Lancaster County." In *Benjamin Franklin, Jonathan Edwards, and the Representatives of American Culture*, edited by Barbara B. Oberg and Harry S. Stout, 186–203. New York: Oxford University Press, 1993.

Lennon, Thomas M., and Paul J. Olscamp, eds. and trans. *The Search after Truth* and *Elucidations of the Search after Truth*. Cambridge: Cambridge University Press, 1997.

Locke, John. *An Essay Concerning Human Understanding*. Oxford: Oxford University Press, 2008.

Lyttle, David J. "The Sixth Sense of Jonathan Edwards." *Church Quarterly Review* 167 (1966) 50–59.

Marsden, George M. *Jonathan Edwards: A Life*. New Haven: Yale University Press, 2003.

———. "Jonathan Edwards in the Twenty-First Century." In *Jonathan Edwards at 300: Essays on the Tercentenary of His Birth*, edited by Harry S. Stout, Kenneth P. Minkema, and Caleb J. D. Maskell, 152–64. Lanham: University Press of America, 2005.

McClymond, Michael J. *Encounters with God: An Approach to the Theology of Jonathan Edwards*. New York: Oxford University Press, 1998.

Miller, Perry. *Errand into the Wilderness*. Cambridge, MA: Harvard University Press, 1956.

———. *Jonathan Edwards*. New York: William Sloane Associates, 1949.

———. *The New England Mind: From Colony to Province*. Cambridge, MA: Harvard University Press, 1953.

Morgan, Edmund S. *Visible Saints: The History of a Puritan Idea*. Ithaca, NY: Cornell University Press, 1963.

Morimoto, Anri. "The End for Which God Created Jonathan Edwards." In *Jonathan Edwards as Contemporary: Essays in Honor of Sang Hyun Lee*, edited by Don Schweitzer, 33–37. New York: Peter Lang, 2010.

Nadler, Steven. *The Cambridge Companion to Malebranche*. Cambridge: Cambridge University Press, 2000.

Nuttall, Geoffrey F. *The Holy Spirit in Puritan Faith and Experience*. Oxford: Basil Blackwell, 1947.

Russell, Bertrand. *A History of Western Philosophy*. New York: Simon & Schuster, 1967.

Schweitzer, Don. "Jonathan Edwards' Understanding of Divine Infinity." In *Jonathan Edwards as Contemporary: Essays in Honor of Sang Hyun Lee*, edited by Don Schweitzer, 49–65. New York: Peter Lang, 2010.

Shedd, William G.T. *Dogmatic Theology*. 3 vols. New York: Charles Scribner's Sons, 1888.

Strobel, Kyle C. *Jonathan Edwards's Theology: A Reinterpretation*. New York: Bloomsbury T&T Clark, 2013.

Ward, Keith. *Rational Theology and the Creativity of God*. Oxford: Basil Blackwell, 1982.

Warfield, B.B. *The Works of Benjamin B. Warfield*, vol. 9. Grand Rapids, MI: Baker, 1981.

Westfall, Richard S. *Never at Rest: A Biography of Isaac Newton*. Cambridge: Cambridge University Press, 1980.

Young, William. "Historic Calvinism and Neo-Calvinism." *Westminster Theological Journal* 36, no. 1 (Fall 1973) 48–64.

———. "Historic Calvinism and Neo-Calvinism." *Westminster Theological Journal* 36, no. 2 (Winter 1974) 156–73.

INDEX

www.ingramcontent.com/pod-product-compliance
Lightning Source LLC
Chambersburg PA
CBHW060341100426
42812CB00003B/1086
* 9 7 8 1 7 2 5 2 5 2 9 2 9 *